The Search for Salvation

David F. Wells

InterVarsity Press
Downers Grove
Illinois 60515

© David F. Wells 1978
First American printing, November 1978,
by InterVarsity Press with permission
from Universities and Colleges Christian
Fellowship, Leicester, England.

InterVarsity Press is the book-publishing
division of Inter-Varsity Christian Fellowship,
a student movement active on campus
at hundreds of universities, colleges and schools
of nursing. For information about local
and regional activities, write IVCF, 233 Langdon
St., Madison, WI 53703.

Distributed in Canada through InterVarsity
Press, 1875 Leslie St., Unit 10,
Don Mills, Ontario M3B 2M5, Canada.

ISBN 0-87784-706-1
Library of Congress Catalog Card
Number: 78-2076

Printed in the United States of America

eology

.... .oward Marshall

The Origins of New Testament Christology
I. Howard Marshall

The Search for Salvation
David F. Wells

To my sons,
Jonathan and David

Acknowledgments

This work could have put on weight as rapidly and easily as does its author. As it is, I have far exceeded the stipulated length. To both the editor and the publisher, then, I must express my immense gratitude for their willingness to publish the manuscript as it stands.

I am grateful, too, to the Board of Trinity Evangelical Divinity School who granted me sabbatical leave during which time much of the work on this book was done, and to my friends and colleagues who read my work in part or in whole and offered their kind criticisms. These include Kenneth Kantzer, Harold Brown, Murray Harris, Walter Kaiser, Sister Agnes Cunningham and Howard Marshall.

For any errors which remain, I accept full responsibility.

Last, but by no means least, I salute my typists Marlene Terbush, Jan Olander and Sue Loop who succeeded, against all odds, in decoding my handwriting.

In law, what plea so tainted and corrupt
But, being season'd with a gracious voice,
Obscures the show of evil? In religion,
What damned error, but some sober brow
Will bless it and approve it with a text,
Hiding the grossness with fair ornament?

William Shakespeare

Religion . . . is the opium of the people. The abolition
of religion as the illusory happiness of the people is a
demand for their true happiness.

Karl Marx

A little philosophy inclineth man's mind to atheism,
but depth in philosophy bringeth men's minds about to
religion.

Francis Bacon

Introduction

The word *save* is not very discriminating about the linguistic company it keeps. Like a lady of the night it wanders through the pages of contemporary print making casual alliances almost at random. Time, fossil fuels, ghettoes, bald eagles, whales, Irish mules, stray cats and money all need to be *saved*, and there are numerous societies, humane and otherwise, who make it their business to *save* them. Without so much as a twinge of conscience it is ready to be co-opted by any cause, be it sacred or profane, high-minded or trivial.

Despite the promiscuous use to which this word lends itself, its meaning in everyday speech is generally clear. To save something means to preserve it, rescue it, reclaim it, deliver it from danger or prevent it from falling into disuse. Its grammatical behaviour is also uncomplicated. All in all, a foreigner is not likely to be confused by beguiling nuances or subtle connotations.

The same, however, cannot be said of its behaviour and meaning in religious discourse. While it is true that there is general agreement that being saved means being preserved, rescued, reclaimed and delivered, there is an extraordinary diversity of views over how this occurs and what its actual consequences are in human life. Paul Minear rightly observed that the 'historian or theologian who seeks honestly to report the ideas of salvation harbored by his religion as a whole may quickly become bogged down in a linguistic and semantic morass'.[1] It is the threat of this quagmire that is both the presupposition of and justification for this study.

Coping with the difficulty

Reducing this semantic confusion to manageable proportions, however, is easier said than done, and the reasons for this should be obvious. First, the doctrine of salvation is so variegated. It draws upon many separate and yet related ideas such as election, the nature of man, sin, the person and work of Christ, the role of the Holy Spirit, grace, faith, atonement, judgment, justification, reconciliation, redemption, conversion, regeneration, sanctification, the sacraments, perseverance and glorification. The literature upon each is great and the present state of discussion is complicated.

Secondly, it is difficult to set workable time limits on the study. The intention of this series of books is to deal with issues in 'contemporary theology'. 'Contemporary' we may conveniently define as meaning the last two to three decades. Even when these parameters are established, however, we are still obliged to deal with parts of the church's more remote past, for the simple reason that the thinkers with whom we are working are recipients of it. Frequently they avail themselves of its accumulated wisdom – and sometimes of its accumulated follies – in fashioning a view of salvation for themselves. Establishing clear time boundaries for the study, therefore, becomes frustrated at every turn as the voice of the past continues to speak in the words of the present and becomes indistinguishable from them.

Thirdly, the underlying presuppositions in the various theological schemes are not always recognized and seldom ever aired, yet it is on these presuppositions that almost everything turns. Differences in *what* theologians hold concerning salvation could be grasped readily if the theologians themselves would state *how* they reached their conclusions. In the absence of such candid self-analysis, the interpreter is left to stumble along as best he can. This problem is particularly acute at two points, those of revelation and the work of Christ. With what presuppositions has the theologian functioned in these two areas?

There are at least two major problems encountered in the idea of biblical revelation. First, what is the exact nature of the revelatory element, and second, what is its relationship to the written text of the Bible? Of the two problems, it is probably the second which has proved more difficult to solve, at least in the period subsequent to the development of biblical criticism. If it can be agreed that God does in some way make a disclosure of himself to men, does he use the written Word to mediate this disclosure? If not, does Scripture have an alternative role to play which is independent of that disclosure?

Like any other theological problem this one has elicited a full range of responses. At one end of the spectrum are traditional Protestants and Roman Catholics who have alike identified the revelatory element with the existent text of Scripture. The differences that divide these two groups are not related to the nature of Scripture but rather to how it is to be interpreted. At the other end of the spectrum are those in the tradition of Protestant liberalism who look on Scripture merely as a shadow of the divine. What Scripture records is not a divinely given revelation in human language but its authors' profound search for God. The searchers were inspired but the text which they wrote is not.

Between these two ends can be found a whole variety of positions which take in elements in differing proportions from each side. Thus, the Barthians generally emphasize the existence of a revelatory Word and scathingly attack the older liberals for having no revelation. On the other hand, like the older liberals they themselves are unwilling to equate this Word with the written Scriptures. Indeed, in his earlier stage Barth declared that this Word could come to a person even as he was reading Karl Marx's *Das Kapital,* but later he became more conservative and insisted that this revelatory insight occurred only in conjunction with the reading or hearing of Scripture. Thus Scripture had for him an important mediatorial role. But this solution did not satisfy some of his disciples who followed Bultmann's lead and adopted more of the liberal elements than had Barth. They severed the Word – the God-given religious perception – from the written Scriptures more or less completely.[2]

There is, in fact, no simple categorization of these views and even where some kind of pattern seems to be emerging, closer inspection has a way of breaking it down. Traditional Protestants, for example, see the element of revelation as coming through the personality of the biblical author and within the operations of his mind. That means that Scripture has to be consulted, not as a telephone directory, but rather as an historical document whose meaning is in part derived through a study of its various cultural environments. By the same token, the liberal Protestantism which showed so much preoccupation with the cultural environments, the personality of each writer and the operations of his mind, was also looking for the presence of revelation. Human and divine elements are present in both of these approaches, as well as in the positions that lie between them, and what is at issue is their relationship. But this does have implications for the way in

11

which a theology is constructed. How is a theologian working? Is he building his views from Scripture, appropriately located and interpreted within its own historic context, or is he working off intuitive insight and if so, what is its relationship to Scripture? The answers to these questions and others like them help an interpreter to see more readily why a writer has taken the position which he has.

With respect to the work of Christ, there are four fundamental issues that are answered one way or another in every doctrine of salvation, whether its author is conscious of having answered them or not. These questions concern the purpose of Christ's work, its nature, how it is made effective and what its results are in human life.

First, what was the *purpose* of Christ's death? There are at least three main possibilities which are not always mutually exclusive. The first of these, *the Latin or penal tradition,* contends that the point of Christ's death was to overcome divine alienation; God, in other words, was its object. Those who so argue do so in terms that are usually penal, seeing God, the fount of all moral purity, as either alienated from man or dishonoured by man's rebellion and law-breaking. Christ's death was designed to reconcile the estranged parties by atoning for sin and assuaging divine wrath, or alternatively by paying the debt which was due and restoring the honour which had been lost.

An alternative to the Latin tradition is the so-called *classic motif.* This sees the devil, rather than God, as the object of Christ's cross-work. In the patristic period, the idea of ransom was used by some to explain this. Satan was seen either as a malicious tyrant or a deceptive usurper who had captured the world and its inhabitants. He demanded as the price of man's release the forfeiture of Christ's life. God, in the person of the Son, undertook the exchange and emancipated the captives. To some modern scholars such as Aulén, this explanation of man's release seemed crude and unattractive but the fundamental notion beneath it was appealing. Discarding the idea of ransom, therefore, they simply maintained that during his life and principally in his death, Christ was locked in combat with the powers of darkness and emerged triumphant.

In contrast to the Latin and classic motifs, is *the Greek or mystical tradition.* This sees the object of Christ's incarnation and death – for the two are conceived together – not as God, still less as the devil, but as man. If sacrificial language is used, it is more as a figure of speech than as implying a penal concept. And if the theme of redemption comes to the surface, it is not in the 'classic' sense of a cosmic duel between God and the devil. Rather, sin is conceived organically as is its remedy. Sin introduced mortality and corruption within man. God, by becoming man, introduced their antidote, immortality and incorruption, enabling man to become God. The scope of this transformation is cosmic and not merely personal. The key thought is divinization, rather than conquest or justification. The purpose of Christ's death, then, can be seen in three entirely different ways depending on whether its prime focus is on God, Satan or man.

Secondly, what was the *nature* of his death? On the one hand, there are those who see it as unique, unlike anything else which happened in his life; on the other hand, there are those who see it merely as the termination of his life, as inspiring and remarkable but not unique. To the first, Jesus' death receives the theological accent and his life is seen as its prelude and presupposition; to the second his death was the final episode in a series of saving activities strung together over thirty years. In the first category are those who maintain the penal view, whether this is conceived transactionally as elaborated by the Protestant Reformers under the doctrine of imputation, the heart of justification, or in the mode of Anselmian satisfaction, according to which Jesus becomes the Ultimate Penitent doing absolutely what men can only do relatively. And loosely related to these ideas, but also in this first category, would be the older proponents of the Governmental theory such as Grotius and Nathaniel William Taylor who argued that God made a token satisfaction of the broken eternal laws through Jesus, thus freeing him openly to forgive all their human violators. In the second category would fall the proponents of the 'classic' theory such as Aulén who see Jesus as being in constant conflict with the powers of darkness, Calvary becoming merely the final and decisive victory. Barth even argues that the first conflict was begun at creation, the incarnate life of Jesus and his death being its continuation and conclusion. Greek Orthodoxy, too, belongs beside these other views, for it sees the saving element as lying, not so much in Christ's death, but more in his life and teaching. His death and resurrection are parts of his life and not uniquely apart from it in terms of theological consequence. A sharp cleavage, therefore, exists between those who see Christ's saving work occurring throughout his life, even if it happens decisively in his death, and those who restrict it to his death, even if his life was its necessary antecedent and indispensable buttress.

Thirdly, how is Christ's work made *effective*? Three main possibilities present themselves. Both Roman Catholics and Greek Orthodoxy, first of all, see the transmission of Christ's saving benefits as reaching men 'physically'. To the former, at least in traditional theology, this occurs through the sacraments, in which that which is signified is mediated through the sign. Thus baptism points to regeneration and is itself regenerative, and the eucharist points to the body of Christ and actually becomes the body of Christ. To the Greek Orthodox, the transmission occurs mystically within humanity. Assumed in this idea is a Platonic ideal of man. Individual people are seen not as isolated and unrelated islands, standing alone in a sea of space, but as integrated aspects of a single, universal Man. The universal, of which each individual is a part, is that to which Christ joined himself in the incarnation and to which he transmitted his immortality and incorruption. If transfiguration or divinization is the end, organic connection with humanity is the means of salvation.[3]

Unlike these proponents of physical union are the old Protestant liberals and the new 'political' theologians for whom Christ's work becomes effective through moral action. Christ's kingdom, of course, is identical neither with the church nor with social institutions, but entry to it is through the quality of one's commitment which may also require active participation in the overthrow of the political order and even violence.

Finally, for those in the historic Protestant tradition, connection with Christ is made, not by sacrament, flesh, morality or political action, but by faith. What is usually assumed is that faith is either generated by the Spirit or at least works through the Spirit. The eternal Spirit of God rather than bare volition provides the continuum or linkage between Christ and the sinner. Christ's work of securing salvation at Calvary and his work now of applying it through the Spirit are seen to belong together. The differences between historic Protestants at this point centre on the relation of faith to the Spirit: is faith the result of the Spirit's work or its cause? There is, however, common agreement that the two elements must be present in some way.

Fourthly, what are the *results* of Christ's work in human life? The factor of religious experience is[4] hard to apply but it does yield some useful insights. Evangelical Protestantism has, perhaps, been most insistent on this factor, describing the sinner's changed relationship before God under the doctrine of justification, and its experience in human life under those of regeneration, conversion, sanctification and finally glorification. Salvation is, therefore, a past event, a continuing process and a future hope. Describing the believer as having died in Christ, it sees Christ living on in the believer's life with the consequence that sin begins to recede. Whether sin can ever be wholly eradicated in this life or whether it will be terminated only in death continues to be debated. All are agreed, however, that Scripture depicts the final act of salvation as a cosmic renovation, a part of which brings believers into a new, purified, heavenly existence.

The factor of experience is present in both Roman Catholicism and Greek Orthodoxy but in different ways and generally with less intensity, the major exception being those in these traditions who are charismatic and who often uphold a view comparable to that of evangelical Protestantism. The former sees grace being imparted to men through the sacraments. Vatican II, however, did not limit this impartation to the sacraments, for even atheists, it taught, can be affected by the grace that, however unrecognized, lies in their hearts. The presence of this grace inclines one to do good works; the reciprocity between the inflow of grace and the active response to it produces the state of existential righteousness, which is justification. In Tridentine theology, only a private revelation could suffice to assure anyone of final salvation, since the question as to whether sin's guilt and debt have been assuaged or not is never normally answered in this life. Recent thought, however, has become extremely muted on the matter of final judgment and there are strong overtones of universalism present. The doctrine of purgatory, consequently, has receded considerably.

The question of religious experience among the neo-orthodox is difficult to pinpoint. How the atonement is conceived to affect people will depend upon two variables, namely the type of sacramental theology which is maintained along with it and the extent to which the 'classic' theory of atonement, which a majority maintain, is modified. Generally speaking, however, there is great concern lest the effectiveness of Christ's work be suspended in any way on the activity of faith, the presence of repentance or the willingness to believe. Neo-orthodoxy stresses what Christ *has* completed; it fears the aspects of subjective appropriation, seeing in these nothing but a covert works doctrine. In as much as it is so emphatically objective in its emphasis, it tends towards universalism and its doctrines of personal conversion, regeneration and sanctification are often so weak as to be almost non-existent.

In the newer theologies of the Third World, especially in South America, the element of personal appropriation, of subjective experience, is deliberately eschewed. Marxist influence is evident, not only in the seedbed of these views in Moltmann's 'theology of hope', but also in the way in which some of these theologians analyse society. Since they define sin in terms of class struggle and class oppression, they are also obliged to see salvation in corporate rather than individual terms. There is, therefore, a concerted effort to 'deprivatize' faith and banish from Christianity the entire element of individual appropriation of Christ's work and of personal relationship to him.

There is, then, a wide diversity of views as to how Christ's work affects human life, ranging all the way from clear insistence on personal religious experience among evangelical Protestants through to a strong insistence that these elements should not be present by the proponents of the 'theology of hope', 'political theology' and 'revolutionary theology'. Between the two poles are to be found Roman Catholics, Greek Orthodoxy and the neo-orthodox, both Lutheran and Reformed. The concept of experience is, however, difficult to explain with precision, more difficult to measure, and subject to variables and modifications so that categorizations such as these have to be somewhat tentative.

Classifying theories

In answering these questions — what are the purpose and nature of Christ's work, how it is made effective and how does it affect human life? — scholars have often found that their answers have fallen into patterns that are more or less self-consistent. How a person answers the questions on nature and purpose should, for example, mesh with how he answers those on how it is made effective and how it affects life. Classifying these patterns, however, is a modern innovation.

Ritschl's *Die christliche Lehre von der Rechtfertigung und Versöhnung*, published in 1872, was the forerunner of these attempts to classify thought on the atonement into self-conscious 'theories.' Ritschl argued that there have been two opposing mentalities in the church from the start. These have their cultural roots, respectively, in the Latin and Greek mind-sets of the patristic period. The Latin West, he argues, always had a tendency to conceive of doctrine in a legalistic fashion, and with respect to the atonement was firmly 'objective' in its view. In Anselm this tendency reached a peak. Sin was defined as withholding one's life from God, which results in debt. Christ's work was seen as satisfying that debt in as much as his life was voluntarily yielded up beyond what was required and so can be seen as a work of supererogation which satisfies the debts of those unable to pay for themselves. It is this tendency to see sin and atonement in a legal framework, to stress the ideas of substitution and sacrifice and to accent the objective side of salvation, that Ritschl saw continuing up through the Reformation and into seventeenth-century scholasticism.

The second doctrinal impetus germinated in the Greek mind, whose concept of sin was always less developed than and different from that of the Latin West. It saw sin, not as debt or legal infraction, but as a clouding of the mind, a weakening of intention. Salvation occurs as much through Christ's teaching, which dissipates the clouds, as through his death, which inspires the will. The accent, therefore, falls on the 'subjective' side of the matter. Ritschl found a convenient contrast in attitudes in the medieval contemporaries, Anselm and Abelard, the former standing for the objective view and the latter for the subjective. Anselm emphasized the fact of original sin and man's built-in propensity to do what is wrong; Abelard denied original sin and pointed to man's inherent capacity to do good. Anselm was concerned with the obstacles which stood in the way to God's forgiveness and which necessitated the giving of the God-man and his cross; Abelard denied any such obstacles and charged the upholders of the Anselmian view with turning God into a blood-thirsty, flinty and unpardoning potentate. Abelard then stressed the willingness of God to forgive without demanding sacrifice and he saw the cross as that which, by its mere contemplation, inspires love for

God in man. This Abelardian theme Ritschl saw emerging in some of the Enlightenment thinkers and especially in Schleiermacher. The issue, therefore, in the modern period has come to this: does the atonement effect a change in God, as the objective tradition has it, or does it effect a change in man as the proponents of the subjective tradition affirm?

Ritschl's delineation held the field more or less intact until 1930 when a Swedish theologian, Gustav Aulén, delivered the Olaus Petri Lectures at Uppsala; these were published the following year and then translated as *Christus Victor*. Aulén's study, he tells us, grew out of 'an ever-deepening conviction that the traditional account of the history of the idea of Atonement [which was Ritschl's] is in need of thorough revision'.[5] Aulén's discomfort with 'the traditional account' was largely over its failure to see what he calls the 'classic' view, the idea that the atonement was neither a legal transaction (the Latin tradition) nor yet an inspiring example of love (the Greek model) but the occasion for a cosmic duel as a result of which Christ overcame the powers of darkness which had held man captive. It is this motif in particular that Aulén saw in Luther, rather than the Latin, legal doctrine, and it is this motif, he believes, which captures biblical teaching on this subject.

Aulén's study has had a profound influence on contemporary theology, but he has not been without his critics. It is sufficient to say here that the typing of atonement theories is considerably more subtle and complex than either Ritschl or Aulén allowed. A great deal sometimes hangs on the subtleties they overlooked.

Limiting the scope

Unfortunately, the scope of this study has had to be limited considerably. It has not been possible to treat the theme of salvation either in contemporary literature[6] or in recent films. A significant area of discourse has thereby had to be excised.

There seems to be little doubt that what Anselm was to the Middle Ages, film directors such as Bergman and Truffaut have become to ours. The shift in the channels of knowledge from the printed page to the celluloid image, no less than the changing influence of that knowledge, has increasingly isolated theology, leaving it beached on the shore of our society like an unwanted and dying whale. The theologian's traditional concerns with meaning, values and how people derive them, continue to be explored and expounded with great effectiveness, not by religious professionals, but by the serious film directors.

It is true, of course, that novelists, like theologians, have to ply their trade by means of the printed page. But they do have one overwhelming advantage. Whereas theologians seem preoccupied with abstruse, speculative concerns, with learned hair-splitting and strife over minutiae, literary people are dealing with 'real life', with flesh and blood concerns, with ordinary people in everyday situations who ache as we all do. If this difference belongs more to appearance than to reality, it still cannot be gainsaid that theologians in the modern period have not communicated well with ordinary people; redemptive themes, consequently, are no longer their exclusive preserve. Salvation is receiving wide and effective treatment in contemporary society but outside of the strict confines of religious discussion and dialogue. The results are often untheological, often nontraditional, but by no means unimportant.

Even within the sphere of technical theology, furthermore, the scope of this study has had to be restricted. It has proved impossible to give an encyclopedic account of each important scheme of salvation in contemporary theology; several volumes would be required to accomplish that task. Instead, a sounding has been taken at regular intervals and the whole has, in this limited and more modest way, been surveyed. It is the difference between Harnack's multi-volumed *History of Dogma* and H. R. Mackintosh's *Types of Modern Theology*.

The two millennia which divide us from New Testament times have seen massive changes in the way people think, organize themselves, live and relate to one another. Empires have collapsed, wars have been fought, treaties have been signed and abrogated. Superstition is retreating before education. The scalpel, syringe and cold analysis of disinterested scientists are permanent factors in our lives. The growth of technology has not, however, been an unmixed blessing. At first it inspired utopian dreams, visions of the world rid of sickness, a world in which evil and suffering were banished. Now, however, the dreams not infrequently seem like nightmares. For ours is a world of nuclear giants and moral infants, a world in which our knowledge has outstripped our capacity to control it. We have manufactured weapons so destructive that a cosmic suicide has become a possibility. And we have the knowhow to tinker with genes and manipulate one another in a barbarically inhuman way. And yet, throughout all of these changes and in the midst of these horrible spectres, biblical teaching has endured, has been believed, and has shaped the values of millions of people. The question asked by the Philippian jailer: 'Sirs, what must I do to be saved?' (Acts 16:30) has been asked in country after country, century after century. It is a question which is neither exclusively ancient nor exclusively modern, but belongs to all seasons and times. In the pages which follow, it is this question that is addressed by the dominant figures in contemporary theology.

Notes

[1] Paul S. Minear, 'Hope of Salvation – Structural Elements in Biblical Soteriology', *Interpretation*, III (July 1949), p. 260.

[2] A brief account of the state of discussion in ecumenical circles is given by James Barr, 'The Authority of the Bible', *The Ecumenical Review*, XXI, No. 2 (April 1969), pp. 135–150; a more extended account can be found in his *The Bible in the Modern World* (London, 1973). The related question is dealt with in David M. Kelsey, *The Uses of Scripture in Recent Theology* (Philadelphia, 1975).

[3] The doctrine of salvation has never been defined authoritatively within Greek or Russian Orthodoxy. In the absence of conciliar action, their doctrine has become that consensus which binds together Irenaeus, Origen, Athanasius, the Cappadocean fathers, Theodoret and John of Damascus. On this tradition see George A. Maloney, *A History of Orthodox Theology Since 1453* (Belmont, 1976) and Vladimir Lossky, *The Mystical Theology of the Eastern Church* (London, 1957). On salvation specifically, see S. Agourides, 'Salvation According to the Orthodox Tradition', *Ecumenical Review*, XXI (July 1969), pp. 190–203; G. B. Sweetland, 'Salvation of the Cosmos in Eastern Christian Tradition', *Journal of Ecumenical Studies*, XII (September 1975), pp. 253–256; Timothy Ware, *The Orthodox Church* (Harmondsworth, 1963), pp. 216–242.

[4] H. D. McDonald, 'What is Meant by Religious Experience', *Vox Evangelica*, II (1963), pp. 58–70.

[5] Gustav Aulén, *Christus Victor: An Historical Study of the Three Main Types of the Idea of Atonement*, trans. A. G. Hebert (New York, 1969: London, 1970). 1. Careful surveys of the atonement in history may be found in L. W. Grensted, *A Short History of the Doctrine of Atonement* (Manchester, 1962); J. K. Mozley, *The Doctrine of the Atonement* (New York, 1916), the second half of which is historical; the same is true of Hastings Rashdall, *The Idea of Atonement in Christian Theology* (London, 1919), though his biases are more evident; Robert S. Franks, *History of the Doctrine of the Work of Christ, in its Ecclesiastical Development* (New York, 1918); Sydney Cave, *The Doctrine of the Work of Christ* (London, 1937); Jean Rivière, *Le dogme de la rédemption dans le théologie contemporaine* (Albi, 1948); the historical sections of Emil Brunner, *The Mediator: A Study of the Central Doctrine of the Christian Faith*, trans. Olive Wyon (Philadelphia, 1947: London, 1967), though aimed largely at Schleiermacher, are very helpful.

[6] On the general relationship between the two see Helen Gardner, *Religion and Literature* (Oxford, 1971); Stuart Barton Babbage, *The Mark of Cain: Studies in Literature and Theology*

(Grand Rapids, 1966: Exeter, 1967); Nathan Scott, *The Broken Center: Studies in the Theological Horizon of Modern Literature* (New Haven, 1966); Nathan Scott, ed., *The Climate of Faith in Modern Literature* (New York, 1964).

Crux sola est nostra Theologia.

Martin Luther

Slain for bringing life;
But to the cross he nails thy enemies,
The law that is against thee, and the sins
Of all mankind, with him there crucified,
Never to hurt them more who rightly trust
In this his satisfaction.

John Milton

Puritanism in its flowering time was a revolution.
Evangelicalism is a counter-revolution.... It tries
instead to harvest the past on the assumption that the
modern is the chaff which the wind driveth away.

Sydney Ahlstrom

Chapter One

Conservative thought

Both Marxism and Freudian psychoanalysis are built on the proposition that the environment determines the man. It is the environment which is corrupt and it is the environment which corrupts. Man's ailments, therefore, need to be assaulted at their source. Marxists see this to be in the prevailing economic order and have dedicated themselves to the overthrow of those who control it, the bourgeois capitalists; Freudians see this as lying in the social structure in which entrenched behavioral patterns thwart the individual's expression of his inward desires. They are dedicated to transforming parental and social relations.

In contrast to these and other philosophies which have also located the source of evil in the outward environment, historic Christianity has always emphasized that the environment is the result, not the cause, of man's corruption and that moral responsibility is individual before it is corporate. Furthermore, since the seeds of decay have been planted first in man's interior life, it is here that he first needs to be redeemed and the outward environment will have little to do with whether or not this takes place.

This does not mean that a person is unaffected by his environment. Undoubtedly the social context in which someone lives shapes his outlook, values, way of life, mental habits, hopes, ambitions and perceptions of the world. These effects are sometimes good and sometimes bad, but whether a person, as a result, is considered a decent and upright citizen or in fact becomes a vicious criminal has no bearing on his need to hear the gospel. In the face of God's command to repent and believe the good news of salvation, all stand on level ground despite the fact that in the social reckoning some occupy the high and others the low points of the scale.

What this means, then, is that man's essential nature is not changed either by time or by circumstances. His way of thinking, his psychology, his values are in motion but the underlying heart stays strangely unchanged. Not least is this true of its guilt. Our cities are symbols of human achievement, but also of human decay, and that type of decay that has always eaten away at our dreams. On our morally fetid streets, people are decomposing. They are no more emancipated from the gnawing pangs of guilt, which are as real as any worm in a corpse, than people ever have been. Neither the perfumes of Arabia nor the accoutrements of the beautiful life can soften this sullen *Angst*. The brash confidence with which we venture into the future is always mocked by the possibility that we may have no future. That very technology that has conquered some of man's worst diseases has also produced the means of our total destruction in atomic, neutron and germ warfare. The weapons change but man's capacity for destruction does not; the dances are different but the orchestra is the same. But how does Christian faith relate to this?

Presuppositions

Conservative theology [1] rests on the twin assumptions of an inspired Bible and the unity of its Testaments[2] which together declare God's unfailing purposes in man's corrupted world. How the Testaments are consistent with one another is usually explained either by appealing to the same divine mind behind each or to the unified divine activities which each records. The first explanation is more static, the second more dynamic; the one lends itself to an older kind of systematizing, the other to newer exegetical concerns.

Working out the integration of the Testaments in practice, however, has not been easy, for conservatives are the recipients of two traditions which, on meeting, create difficult tensions. On the one hand, conservatives generally see themselves as the heirs to a heritage of thought that begins decisively in Augustine at least, was handed down through the Reformers, continues into Puritanism and moves down to the present. Its fundamental presuppositions are an inspired Bible (the unflawed authenticity of its writings being the result) and the centrality of salvation as the unifying theme of its two Testaments. On the other hand, conservatives are increasingly demonstrating their proficiency in and knowledge of the contemporary world of biblical scholarship, the prevailing assumptions of which are that the biblical text is not so inspired and its unifying theme, if it has one, is not salvation, at least as this has been traditionally expounded by the theologians. How these two impulses are to be reconciled is not always clear.

The field can, of course, be limited to some extent. The complete disjuncture that Rudolf Bultmann posits between the Testaments, his relegation of the Old to the category of failure and his sole preoccupation with the New as alone relevant, has not commended itself to conservatives. Likewise, one-sided proposals which insist that the New is simply a glossary to the Old, or that the Old is encapsulated and exhaustively contained in the New also cause difficulties because they violate the self-contained integrity of each of the Testaments. In a different way, the same result is achieved when the many-sided teaching of the Testaments is reduced to any one controlling theme, in the application of which an emasculation of other biblical substance takes place. This has occurred under a variety of contexts but perhaps nowhere more ruthlessly than among those influenced by neo-orthodoxy, for they have pursued single-mindedly their christomonistic motif to the disparagment of other matters contained in the biblical revelation.[3]

Traditionally, of course, there have been basically two schools within conservative thought which, in struggling with the problems of relating the Testaments, have come to rather different conclusions. The distinctives of these schools have significantly affected the way that salvation has been conceived.

The first approach is that of dispensationalism, pioneered by J. N. Darby, popularized by Scofield's Bible, defined by Lewis Sperry Chafer[4] and modified recently by Charles Ryrie. It sees seven different periods in God's dealings with men and distinguishes within these, four separate gospels: the gospel of the kingdom, the gospel of grace, the everlasting gospel and Paul's gospel. At the core of the system is the first one, the gospel of the kingdom, the content of which is the promise, not yet fulfilled and never abrogated, that God will establish an earthly kingdom for Israel as promised in the Davidic covenant.[5] This kingdom, unlike that of the present gospel age of grace, will be established by divine power, not human persuasion; will be a rule of law, not of grace; will be established by Christ as king, not as priest; and will embrace the greater part of mankind, not the customary

25

minority. Given the disjuncture between Christ as king and priest, between gospels of law and grace and between the multiple relations God establishes with men across the ages, it is difficult to resist the criticism of O. T. Allis[6] that this solution, while honouring the inspiration of Scripture, sets the Testaments against one another and undercuts the very unity it is supposed to be securing.

The second approach has been developed around the notion of the covenant. John Murray, for example, defines a covenant (*berit* or *diathēkē*), not merely as a compact between equal and consenting parties, but as God's establishment of a relationship of grace which carries moral obligations for its human recipients.[7] These covenants – principally the Noahic (Gn. 9:9–17), Abrahamic (Gn. 17:1–8), Mosaic (Ex. 6:6–8; 4:22, 23; 2:24, 25; 19:5–8), Davidic (Ps. 132:11–18) and the 'new covenant' (Gal. 3:17–22; Mt. 26:28; 2 Cor. 3:6–18; Heb. 9:16, 17) – are soteriological in intent, universal in scope, irrevocable in their nature and inviolate in their outworkings. What unites the Testaments is their common record of God's sovereign initiative in saving a people for himself according to his unbroken and unbreakable covenants. The objective means of realization in the Old Testament were provisional, namely the prophetic and priestly channels; the core of the covenants, however, is the same in both Testaments. 'There is but one, unified testament,' writes Barton Payne, 'God's sole plan of salvation, through which Christ offers a redemption that is equally effective for the saints of both dispensations.'[8] There is, despite the elements of discontinuity, one gospel and not four, one *dispensatio* of grace and not seven. Likewise, R. K. Harrison, in a massive study, sums up this approach by saying that 'although the theological concepts of the Old Testament do not lend themselves with particular readiness to attempts at systematization, as Eichrodt conceded, there can be little doubt that the covenant idea must be given an important place in any formulation of the unity of Scripture.'[9]

The most common criticisms of the covenant solution to testamental unity are that it is insensitive to the different relations that God has established with men and that it is too constricted in its scope, for the Bible is more than a treatise on grace. The first criticism is only as valid as is dispensationalism. The second can probably be met by arguments advanced by F. F. Bruce, Francis Foulkes and Walter Kaiser.[10] Bruce integrates the Testaments in terms of common themes such as 'the people of God' and 'the victory of God'. Foulkes sees the integration to be in certain divine 'acts', biblically interpreted, which recur in a typological pattern. The Old Testament, he argues, looked to God to re-enact in the future his great acts of judgment and grace from the past. It looked forward to. a more glorious David, Moses, Elijah and Melchizedek, an exodus whose deliverance would be even greater,[11] another and more awesome Passover, a new temple, new acts of creation and a 'more glorious' covenant. What the Old Testament hoped for, the New declares has happened. This is a typology neither allegorical nor fanciful, which allows Scripture itself to make clear where the type and antitype lie and sees these largely in God's saving acts rather than in people or institutions. Kaiser has developed a notion of integration around the idea of the promise doctrine which similarly links Old Testament hope with New Testament realization. These solutions should be seen as variations on the covenant idea, which give it a clearer sense of historical development and provide a broader base for connecting the Testaments. They are also sensitive to and capitalize upon the genuine gains of recent biblical scholarship.

The Christian understanding of salvation, conservatives believe, needs to be placed in this broader context; narrow semantic studies are useful so far as they go, but they often do not go far enough.[12] For it is not difficult to see that in Jesus' teaching the Old Testament understanding of salvation has been assumed and deepened, and parts of it made more explicit.[13] The Old Testament conviction, for example, that it is *God,* rather than man himself, who saves is carried over into Jesus' teaching in the connection he made between salvation (*soteria*) and the kingdom, the latter being that spiritual sphere which God establishes and over which he reigns. In the Old Testament, salvation is received and in Jesus' teaching the kingdom is entered, simply by trust. In both, God is seen to save, not in the abstract, but within the concrete historical process. The Old Testament records many such 'acts', although the exodus was the most memorable, and this same thought came to force in Jesus' teaching of God's intent to save through the earthly Son of man. In both, salvation is costly to God. In the Old Testament this was stated simply and directly; towards the end of Jesus' ministry it was made explicit in his teaching that the Son of man must suffer vicariously for his people.[14] Salvation

27

is seen in both Testaments as rescue from one's enemies, but in the Old these were frequently foes that were external and physical, whereas in Jesus' sayings they are usually internal and spiritual. And in both, salvation brings wholeness to body and soul, producing spiritual triumph and bringing a vindication to faith. There are, then, many points at which Jesus' teaching on salvation meshes with that of the Old Testament, the differences arising only where he deepens it, in some respects internalizes it, and then makes explicit that the means of its realization is in the sacrificial death of the Son of man.[15]

This same framework of understanding continues through the rest of the New Testament, although it was Paul who made it his business especially to elaborate upon this tradition, enlarging it without contradicting or subverting it.[16] He is convinced that the coming of Jesus has brought the awaited eschatological future of Jewish expectation into the present. While Paul sometimes uses 'salvation' of a past event, he is far more prone to speak of it as a present experience and as a future hope. The initiative in salvation is ascribed to God, the ground of it to his grace, the means of it, objectively, to the life, death and resurrection of Jesus and, subjectively, to faith seen merely as a channel of reception. The enemy from which Christians are saved is again understood spiritually rather than physically. Believers are saved from the old aeon (sin, law, wrath and death), the old state (conformity to a godless world), the old fears (despair, dread, *Angst*) and from the old habits (acquiescence in sinful worldliness).[17]

Salvation in the past

With respect to salvation as a past event, Paul uses three additional word 'models'[18] to give further precision to his over-arching concept of salvation.[19] These words, redemption (*apolutrōsis*), reconciliation (*katallassō*) and justification (*dikaioō*) are distinguished from *sotēria* but never separated from it. They magnify parts of the general theme of salvation rather than being departures from it.

Both inside and outside the New Testament, Leon Morris argues, *apolutrōsis* means deliverance from captivity at the payment of a price.[20] It is *God* who must deliver man, for man can neither free himself from his captors nor pay the price of his guilt. And it is this theme in particular which has for obvious sociological reasons provided blacks in North America with their basic understanding of salvation, their theology being fashioned not in the technical language of academia but in song.[21]

The verbs *apokatallasso* and *katallasso* as applied to Christ's death are metaphors drawn, of course, not from the slave market, but the domain of human relations.[22] Reconciliation presupposes a prior estrangement between two parties, an estrangement that has been overcome and healed. In Pauline thought, man is alienated from God by sin and God is alienated from man by wrath. It is in the substitutionary death of Christ that sin is overcome and wrath averted, so that God can look on man without displeasure and man can look on God without fear. Sin is expiated and God is propitiated.

Morris is insistent that propitiation, the *hilaskomai* word group, cannot be translated as 'expiation' which, in fact, is not even used in Scripture.[23] The major incentive to do so has been the fear that the attribution of anger to God, which the word *propitiation* implies, is unworthy and un-Christian. Yet Morris stands on substantial Christian ground in insisting that this is not so.[24] If the anger of God is seen to be defiled by the same imperfections that normally accompany human anger such as malice, envy, passion and vindictiveness, then it is, indeed, hard to sustain as a Christian idea. If, however, it is seen as God's final resistance to wickedness, as the deep and relentless opposition of good to evil, as the means by which truth is finally enthroned and error condemned to the scaffold, then it is exactly what a Christian might expect of his saving God. The wrath of God understood in this fashion actually undergirds all Christian moral behaviour, for if evil rather than good is to triumph there is no reason to live ethically and every reason not to.[25] Because the New Testament is so insistent on the performance of high moral standards, it is so frequently eschatological.

The third metaphor, contained within the *dikaioo* word group, has reference to the law court and has to do with being freed from guilt and condemnation.[26] Justification is the act by which God declares sinners freed of blame because of the interposition of his Son who not only absorbs and exhausts their due judgment but provides a righteousness alien to those in whose place he stands. It has to do with righteousness declared by objective pardon rather than imparted by existential encounter. God does indeed reconstitute human nature subjectively, but this, in the Bible, is subsumed under the doctrines of regeneration and sanctification; neither, however, can occur in isolation from the reckoning with broken law that must be made. Justification, therefore, is that act by which divine love upholds the cause of divine justice and the costliness of the action is as much a token of the inviolability of his law as it is of the persistence of his love. In justifying the guilty God himself must be 'justified'.

There is little doubt in the mind of conservative thinkers that the New Testament sees substitution[27] as being inextricably a part of reconciliation, redemption and justification. Jesus not only dies for the world, for all men, for his sheep, but he bears their sin and penalty, standing in their place under divine judgment, overcoming the alienation between God and men, rescuing men from the captivity of sin, death and the devil, doing for them what they could never do and will never be required to do for themselves. And they, identified with him in faith, die with him in his death, pass under its covering through judgment, and rise with him into the newness of his resurrection life.[28]

The idea of substitution and, in particular, of penal substitution has, however, fallen on hard times in modern theology, the objections to it being generally of two sorts. First, there are the reiterations of the old arguments most clearly put forth originally by Socinus that this idea is unjust, for the guilty escape and an innocent person is condemned. Furthermore, Socinus claimed that it is irreligious, for it excludes both real forgiveness when it demands its price and real faith since a satisfaction made cannot be withdrawn in the absence of trust. This line of reasoning has been met decisively by J. I. Packer[29] who points out that the mysterious transactions occurring in the death of Christ are explained in the New Testament by metaphoric 'models' — the slave market, human relations, the law court — which should put readers on notice that the interpretations and the event are related to one another analogously.[30] The biblical explanations are true but incomplete. They describe the *nature* of the atonement, not its mechanics. To insist on prying open what has not been revealed — how precisely it works — is, Packer argues, the trademark of the rationalist. The second objection is that the idea of the law court with God as its judge and the sinner as its criminal is not derived from the New Testament and has the unfortunate effect of depersonalizing man's relationship to God because it builds on legal maxims. But those who argue that the legal motif is absent from the New Testament betray an unfamiliarity with its language; the more important question, assuming its presence, is what it means. A great many analogies from human law have, traditionally, been employed to explain this but Packer counters that these really miss the point for they are all explanations as to *how* the atonement works. Instead, the law motif establishes that the personal divine-human relationship occurs within a moral framework, that sinful infractions of the law cannot be cancelled by making amends and that the penalty necessitated by the broken law is borne by God himself. It is a motif rather than a theory, explaining the atonement's nature rather than its inward functioning.[31] Accepting a penal motif, however, does not oblige us to accept uncritically the entire Latin view of atonement.

It is Gustav Aulén's contention that the Latin theory of atonement sees Christ doing absolutely what men can only do relatively, that is offering satisfaction to God for the broken law. The movement is from man to God rather than from God to man. It is so because Christ stands in the place of men doing what they ought to do; he is not standing in the place of God destroying man's captors for what they have done.[32]

Aulén has in mind the notion of *satisfactio* originated by Tertullian and elaborated by Anselm, whose *Cur Deus Homo?* is virtually considered a blueprint for the Latin view. What Aulén has not seen is that there were two ideas connected with Tertullian's notion of *satisfactio*, only one of which Anselm developed, the other being purified later and articulated by the Reformers. What this means is that the Latin theory is susceptible to two different interpretations, depending on how *satisfactio* is being understood; Aulén reduces the two to one and that to Anselm's.

First, Tertullian argued that sin incurs debt which a Christian, having received baptism, is obliged to negate through penance.[33] Anselm assumed this idea but modified it by insisting that the debt so incurred has infinite consequences which only an infinite person can obliterate. Christ, therefore, offers to God representatively and in behalf of men what they could not offer efficaciously by and for themselves. Secondly, Tertullian asserted that in the act of penance what would have been an eternal punishment is transmuted and

31

commuted into a temporal one.[34] It was this thought which the Protestant Reformers, including Luther, purged and applied to Christ's death, seeing him as paying our eternal debt in time. Their reinterpretation of the Latin theory, which continues to provide the stuff of contemporary conservative thought, is a dramatic picturing of God's triumphant action against sin, judgment, death and the devil which combines what Aulén insists on sundering, namely, penal and classic motifs. The assuaging of divine retribution is the very means of the triumph heralded in the classic idea, for man's spiritual foes hold him captive not by force but through man's standing alliance with sin. Once this bond is severed, man is free.

Salvation in the present

The present experience of salvation in its moral aspects is comprehended under the doctrine of sanctification in the New Testament, the basic word group having to do with 'being separated'. Early Christians were familiar with this idea for it had a long Old Testament lineage. God had separated the sabbath, the temple, the priests and the nation itself. No person or institution could be separated merely by human consecration. The right to separate belonged to God alone and what he separated was called holy, not because of its intrinsic worth, but because it was ministrant to his special purposes. In the New Testament, Christians are seen as separated, as 'holy', as 'saints', not because of their intrinsic purity but because they serve God's purposes. They are temples and priests, their lives are to be like a sabbath and they are members of an elect nation. If a Christian has been sanctified, he must, however, go on being sanctified; he has put on the new man, but he must go on doing so; he has crucified the old nature, but it must be crucified continually. The difference in the tenses is the difference between 'positional' and 'conditional' sanctification. This experiential aspect of sanctification has been interpreted within conservative thought in three rather different ways, each of the patterns having historic antecedents and contemporary variants. These are the Wesleyan, the Reformed and the Pentecostal-charismatic.

John Wesley himself provided the core of later Wesleyan thought when he explained sanctification as love 'expelling sin', as pure love dominating the heart and life, excluding every 'wrong temper', and controlling 'all thoughts, words and actions'. That many Christians experience this only spasmodically, he readily acknowledged. The problem, he countered, was that though regenerate these Christians had not entered into the 'second change'. This crisis involved the 'destruction' of what he called 'the old man' or 'the carnal mind'. Between regeneration and this experience of 'entire sanctification', it was possible to weaken sin by self-discipline and moral effort, but complete victory could not be had until sin was extirpated completely. This second experience, entered into largely by faith and 'remotely' by repentance is what others then and since have called Christian perfection. Wesley himself was wary of all such 'pompous' names for the experience. Within the New Testament itself, he pointed to John among the apostles as showing indisputable evidence of being entirely sanctified. Wesley's doctrine is drawn largely from the Johannine writings, although he said it was also consistent with the 'whole tenor of the New Testament'. The critical sections for this view are 1 John 1:7–9; 3:6–9 and 5:18, which, it is believed, hold out the hope that Christians can be saved from *all* sin.[35]

If sanctification as the experience of divine love, and perfection, its result, are Wesleyan themes, Reformed thought has tended to focus upon the Pauline concept of strife within the self, the key passages being Galatians 5:16–26 and Romans 7:7–25.[36] The frustrating oscillation between the 'flesh' and the 'spirit' is contrary to God's law but will continue until death, subject, however, to a 'progressive displacement of the old by the new nature'. The inward conflict of Romans 7, therefore, is descriptive not merely of the unregenerate person but also of the regenerate.

In Wesleyan thought the 'second change' is moral in its emphasis. In the Pentecostal-charismatic tradition, the third of the interpretations being considered, the emphasis is more emphatically experiential and in Pentecostalism it is usually termed the 'second blessing'. In earlier Pentecostal teaching, much of it strongly influenced by the Holiness movements, the 'baptism of the Spirit' was predicated upon an experience of 'entire sanctification'. In recent years this has faded within Pentecostalism and it is hardly evident at all within the broader charismatic movement. At the centre of the teaching now is the idea that all Christians should receive a spiritual baptism, that this experience is subsequent to and not to be confused with regeneration, that its purpose is the giving of needed power for witness and evangelism and that the usual evidence of its reception is glossolalia. This baptism, it is argued, is promised in Acts 1:5 and can be discerned within the book of Acts in the biographies of people who received it subsequent to regeneration.[37]

The differences between the traditions raise interesting questions of methodology, for while each maintains that it believes what all of Scripture teaches, it can be discerned that each has found in a particular part of the New Testament a 'key' to the other parts. For Reformed thought, the Pauline corpus gives the paradigm; for Wesleyan teaching it is the Johannine, for the charismatic it is the book of Acts.

It is appropriate to question, however, whether an interpreter can legitimately use a historical book such as Acts to serve this role, laying an interpretive grid over the doctrinal letters. The doctrinal letters, especially those of Paul and John, have different emphases, but they plainly do not diverge as much as their interpreters do in the Reformed and Wesleyan traditions. It follows, then, that there may be within these latter traditions practitioners of honest and rigorous exegesis who are, as a result, far closer to one another on this matter of sanctification than they might have realized.

Salvation in the future

The future aspect of salvation is made up of a series of inter-related but highly complex doctrines within the New Testament corpus. These doctrines are related to the present experience of salvation as the whole is to some of its parts, for while it is true that Christ is present in the world now, paradoxically he is also yet to come. Full redemption has been received but redemption has not been received in full.

The details of Christ's return[38] are debated with considerable feeling, especially in North America. The main option is between premillennialism and amillennialism, since post-millennialism, which was favoured by an earlier generation, has few adherents today. Premillennialism is a consistent outworking of dispensationalism as amillennialism is of covenant theology, but not all premillennialists are dispensational and not all covenant theologians are amillennial. The debate is over how much of Old Testament eschatological expectation has been realized in the New Testament, how much has been realized spiritually and whether there are aspects yet to be realized apart from the actual return of Christ himself. The differences come to focus in particular on whether Israel has a national future within the saving purposes of God. Premillennialism sees Israel's present reconstitution as possibly the beginning of a train of events that will culminate in the establishment of Christ's earthly rule and then his judgment of the world. The alternative in amillennialism is to see the promises made to national Israel already realized in the spiritual 'new Israel' and therefore to look, not for a complex configuration of world events, but only for a sudden, abrupt conclusion to the world's life with the glorious appearing of Christ.

Salvation in the future has to do with being with Christ, sharing his presence, being ushered into his life, abandoning forever the final vestiges of sin and receiving a new resurrection body. Whether all Christians can look forward with unqualified certainty to this future has been debated.[39] On the one hand, there are those who have pointed to the warnings in Scripture against apostasy and 'falling away', and who have concluded that the presence of an active faith is the condition of the Christian's continuation of his relationship to Christ. On the other hand, there have been those who have built their view on those other statements denying that God's saving purposes can be frustrated even by human fecklessness. They have therefore concluded that Christ's cross was sufficient to forgive and is efficacious in forgiving, nor merely the sins that lie behind justification, but also all those which lie beyond it up to the moment of glorification, including that of apostasy. It is not possible for a Christian to be lost. God will persevere with him to the very end. Both sides are agreed that the norm for a Christian is the exercise of continuing, lively faith; both are agreed on the sinfulness of lapsing from grace at any point and in the serious loss which will result from doing so. They differ as to whether this loss can be exclusion from Christ's presence and whether the warnings on falling away assume the possibility that this can happen.

Christians in society

Salvation is not, however, a narrowly religious affair which centres only upon interior attitudes. At its centre it is undoubtedly an experience of God and of his grace, but this experience carries with it the dynamic for seeing things and people in a totally different light.

Take, for example, the matter of daily work. Our society, like societies at other times in the modern period, sees work and its material rewards as ends in themselves. People work because they need and want money; that is the point of each day's activity. And in our industrialized and materialistic society, the importance of the work done is reflected in the recompense which is given. From this arrangement, however, spring those *social* distinctions – based on the type of work done and the salary which is drawn – according to which some people are less important and others more important. Indeed, even in those Marxist societies where these social consequences have been so scathingly denounced and the matter of recompense radically changed, it is not evident that any other rationale for work has yet emerged. The debate between Marxists and capitalists in this regard is not over the nature of work but over who will get the money, how it will be distributed.

Conservative Christians are generally uncomfortable with these social distinctions, too, and with good reason. For God, the Scripture declares, is no respecter of persons and simply brushes the social hierarchy aside. He is apparently unconcerned that the church is often composed of the ungifted, the ordinary, and those without a trace of blue blood in their veins (1 Cor. 1:26–31; Jas. 2:1–12). If the social hierarchy is irrelevant to him, it ought to be irrelevant to his people. The problem, however, is to know how to translate this perception into practical life in each and every case.

The root cause of this drive to arrange people on a scale of importance is obviously the concept of work. Consequently, those in the Reformation traditions have always contended that work is also a *means* and not only an end. It is a means to the expression of the person's spirituality (Eph. 6:6). It is service rendered to God if it is done in the right spirit, no matter how seemingly 'secular' the activity is. Those in the Reformed[40] and Anglican[41] traditions have worked this out on the basis of the creation and the cultural mandate in

Genesis 1:28, 29, while those in the Lutheran tradition[42] have developed it more commonly under the rubric of 'vocation'. The thought, however, is the same. In order to work for God and to live an ethically significant life, one does not need to retreat into a monastery. On the contrary, this can be achieved in one's 'vocation' even if — to take Luther's extreme example — one is called upon to be a hangman. Monasticism has never been an option for evangelical Christians because of their perception that it is in the work of the real world and, in particular, in the home that the values of the sermon on the mount (Mt. 5:1–7:28) must be learned and practised.

These values, however, have proved easier to live out attitudinally than they have in terms of hard, social realities. If the Christian, as the bearer of these values, is to be salt and light in his society, what kind of economic changes, for example, should he hope to see? In many of the countries of the Third World and some countries in Europe, conservatives have often keyed their economic outlook to the perception that our social distinctions are essentially fraudulent. The economic system, therefore, should be geared to overcoming them by securing maximum employment, a working wage for all, and a system of taxation that draws from each according to his ability to pay and redistributes to each according to his need. In North America and among some British thinkers, however, a different attitude is evident. While the various forms of socialism may seem more Christian in theory, they are always rendered unworkable, the argument goes, by the presence of sin. It is this which explains the generally poor performance of socialist economies. It is far better and more Christian, it is countered, to recognize the reality of our fallen world. North Americans, therefore, more commonly argue for a strong free enterprise system in which sin is checked, not by proliferating governmental regulations, but by open competition in the market place. Undoubtedly this system produces higher unemployment and more obvious injustices to those who cannot compete and do not succeed, but it is argued that this is less offensive than the mass penalization and undermining of personal responsibility which is necessitated in socialism. These are exceedingly complex issues, but it has to be said that the level of desire among conservatives to live out a biblical worldview has not always been matched by a comparable wisdom in knowing how to do it.

It has become more apparent in recent years, though, that conservatives have been struggling deeply with other aspects of their relationship to society. Summing up this growing concern, the Lausanne Congress, held in 1974, declared: 'The message of salvation implies also a message of judgment upon every form of alienation, oppression and discrimination, and we should not be afraid to denounce evil and injustice wherever they exist.'[43]

Yet again it is not altogether clear what the relationship is between the preaching of the verbal gospel and the social action which is urged. In Britain, social action is being increasingly seen as the necessary *context* of the spoken message, the two being yoked together under the single mission of God in the world.[44] In North America, however, social action is more commonly seen only as the *consequence* of the preached message, and there is considerable apprehension over the possibility that the two might be confused. This is understandable. First, North American conservatives still nurse painful memories of their clashes with the social gospel movement. There is no doubt that in America the good news of salvation was lost in and obscured by the liberals' concern with social action. Secondly, there are probably cultural reasons for this difference, too. Those who are amenable to socialism will problably have a natural affinity for social action; those who believe that capitalism, despite its flaws, is the best of the systems will accent the kind of personal responsibility which that system requires and to which the preached gospel appeals.

This growing concern to relate the news of salvation to people in such a way that they will not only hear of the love of God but see it exemplified is hardly a novel aspect of conservative thought. Although it is not widely recognized, this was actually a prominent aspect of the life of the Reformation churches, and certainly the achievements of eighteenth-century evangelicalism are well known. Despite recent attempts to denigrate the role played by evangelical Christians during the Wesleyan revival, there seems little doubt that they, almost single-handedly, were responsible for the abolition of the slave trade, the liberation of the slaves, the reform of Britain's barbaric penal code and prison system, and the introduction of a mass of laws to protect the poor and weak from exploitation during the Industrial Revolution.[45] Furthermore, the social concern expressed by foreign missionaries during the centuries which have followed, their work on behalf of the poor, the suffering and the outcast, has often been nothing less than spectacular.[46] It may be true, however, that the social work of the missionaries has been far more pronounced and more readily accepted than that of the home churches from which they have been sent. So if evangelicals stand in a solid tradition of Christian social concern, it also is true that much more still needs to be done in this regard especially within the western democracies themselves.

Returning, however, to the intellectual side of the matter, it should probably be said that the most obvious characteristic of conservative theology today is its sketchy, tentative state. After all, where are the children of Charles Hodge, A. A. Hodge, B. B. Warfield, Abraham Kuyper, Herman Bavinck, James Denney, James Orr, Griffith Thomas, John Theodore Mueller, William Shedd, Thomas Dabney, Franz Pieper, Lewis Sperry Chafer, A. H. Strong and Louis Berkhof? There are virtually none. The sole representative of any standing of this tradition of doing theology is Gerrit Berkouwer although Helmut Thielicke has worked on its fringes, and on a more modest literary scale Carl Henry, Clark Pinnock, John Murray and J. I. Packer belong within it, too. In the absence of fresh and creative theological work, conservatives have tended either to rely on the reprinted works of the older theologians or to eschew the business of doing technical theology altogether, often seeing C. S. Lewis' writings as pointing to the most desirable way of fashioning a Christian world-view.

This does not mean, of course, that conservative scholars have been idle. They have, in fact, expended a great deal of effort in recent years, not in the production of comprehensive systematic theologies, but in careful exegetical studies, often of a highly erudite nature. To some extent this work has been taken up into the recent volumes on 'biblical theology' but it remains true that the word *theology* in a conservative context has a rather vacuous meaning.

The easiest way to see this is to draw a distinction between doctrine and theology. Allowing for conservative assumptions, doctrine is the straightforward summary of what the Bible teaches on any subject; it is the sum of Christian convictions as these arise from Scripture. Theology should be an extension of and an elaboration upon doctrine. It should be the secondary reflection on the content of biblical doctrine. Doctrine and theology should be related, not as adjacent disciplines, but as the first step is to the second in the same process. Theology should be concerned to organize doctrines, explore their relations, expose their problems, defend their teaching, relate their content to other fields of knowledge and apply their conclusions to each age in a philosophical and cultural vernacular native to it.

Theology, in other words, is what roots doctrine in any particular age. For example, it is possible to show that the biblical doctrine of atonement is built around a number of motifs two of which might be seen as central, the penal and the classic. The former, which is concerned with the idea of punishment, obviously assumes the existence of fixed eternal laws and of a Judge who presides over the moral structure of the world and upholds its laws. These are assumptions which were once widely maintained far beyond the borders of Christian faith. Today, however, they find little acceptance outside Christian circles. Secularism refuses to consider as relevant any antecedent principles and metaphysical commitments; it is empirical in its outlook, refusing to place everyday events and decisions in a supernatural framework. The constituents of secularism are varied and numerous, such as evolutionary ideals, naturalism, humanism, pragmatism and materialism, but the upshot of it all is that the biblical doctrine of justification and its celestial courtroom simply does not make sense.

The same, however, cannot be said of the conquest motif contained in such texts as Luke 11:20; 1 John 5:19; 3:8; John 12:31; 16:11; Galatians 1:4; 1 Corinthians 15:26; Colossians 2:15 and Hebrews 2:14. The idea of man's soul being both the battleground and the prize for supernatural contestants – God and the devil, Christ and anti-Christ, the Lamb and the dragon – is immediately comprehensible to the modern mind, and theology can find an easy *entreé* for doctrine at this point. For almost by common consent, modern man sees himself caught in a mammoth struggle that far transcends the dimensions of private doubt. The individual has the feeling of being pitted against unseen forces which consistently rob him of his authenticity. This is the gist of much of the existential analysis of the human condition which holds true politically as well; for in the Marxist lands, for example, there is an omnicompetent State, conceived to be ministrant to principles inherent in history, but whose tentacles not merely embrace each and every citizen but also throttle him. And even in the so-called 'free world' there is such a pervasive sense of calamity, such a fracturing of self-identity that it seems natural always to talk about 'us' and 'them'. The idea, then, that man is captive to forces which he might not be able to see but whose hold over him is nevertheless real is immediately comprehensible. Presumably that is why a film such as *The Exorcist* aroused such a response, despite the fact that twentieth-century sophisticates are not supposed to believe in devil possession. Less obviously but probably just as really, the makers of *Jaws*, the story of a great white shark's attacks just off the New England coast, were able to tap the same fears. The shark's attacks were ruthless and unpredictable, merciless and unerring. It was seemingly invincible and chillingly efficient in its work of destruction. There could be no better symbol for the unseen forces which bind and assault people today with the same kind of irrationality and yet of chilling efficiency, forces seldom ever seen and yet from whom escape is impossible.

The task of theology, then, might be in part to explore and analyse the modern mind and develop ways of linking it to the biblical doctrine of Christ's conquest over the devil in whose chilling grasp the whole world is held. Once the contact is established it becomes much easier to show that the captivity is not, as seemed at first sight, merely a matter of blind power, or of impersonal structures or of pure political ideology, but it is essentially moral and religious in nature. Christ delivers people from this tyranny by 'disarming' the powers of darkness, revealing the nature of their deception of people, releasing from the bonds of sin those who trust him, reversing the inward disintegration of their nature, breaking open their prison brought on through death, and cancelling their penalty.

There is, therefore, an element both of continuity and of discontinuity in Christian belief. The former is constituted by the biblical doctrine, the *depositum fidei,* which should be handed on inviolate from generation to generation. This is the true apostolic succession, in which believers continue to accept what the apostles taught, as opposed to the idea that apostolic succession involves the transmission of ecclesiastical powers to succeeding generations of bishops. It is a succession of doctrine, not of authority. The element of discontinuity appears when doctrine is rooted in any age, when theologians utilize contemporary notions either to defend it or to interpret it meaningfully. Theology is always and inescapably a work of 'enculturation' and therefore no theology is durable. Doctrine never changes, but theology, which places a shell around the nut, does. Doctrine abhors novelty; theology in both its defensive and interpretive roles, requires it.

Establishing the right relationship between doctrine and theology is what modern thought has discovered to be one of its most stubborn and intractable problems. Roman Catholics, for example, have worked hardest at reconciling the elements of stability and change. Their solution, derived principally from Newman, is, however, unsatisfactory. For while they have acknowledged that new elements have arisen, instead of assigning these to the domain of theology which is always ministrant and subservient to biblical doctrine, they have assigned these to doctrine. Later changes in belief are said to be the worked-out implications of the *depositum fidei,* regardless of whether the development is elaborated logically (an older emphasis) or simply perceived intuitively (the new emphasis). In effect, theology is being put on a par with doctrine rather than standing perpetually under its judgment. This is the only explanation for the acceptance of certain soteriological ideas, such as Mary as Co-redemptrix and Mediatrix, about which Scripture explicitly says nothing and which it implicitly outlaws in advance.

Within Protestantism, the attempt to unite doctrine and theology, what is continuous with what is not, has more or less been abandoned. On the one side are those who have found it difficult, if not impossible, to do theology within the constraints of biblical doctrine. On the other side are those conservatives who have found it difficult and seemingly unnecessary to advance beyond exegesis into the interpretive realm. The former have theology without doctrine, and the latter doctrine without theology.

In practice, of course, the distinction is never quite as clean as this, for there is always a smattering of doctrine in every theology, otherwise it would cease to be Christian even in name, and conservatives always do a modicum of theology even when they imagine they are doing only exegesis. Doctrine and theology appear together, and the difference is usually one of degree. The failure to recognize this has produced a great deal of mischief. Those who are not conservative have a tendency to ascribe to biblical doctrine the relativity that attaches to their own theology and the biblical authors are simply seen as doing what these theologians are concerned with, namely spinning a philosophy of life. On the other hand, conservatives have a tendency to ascribe to their efforts in theologizing the absolute authority that belongs only to biblical doctrine. In the aftermath of the modernist controversy, for example, the 'satisfaction view' of Christ's death was seen to be an essential part of an acceptable orthodoxy. This was, however, a theological venture designed to protect a biblical doctrine. As such it often went far beyond the simple statements of the Bible to do its work, utilizing elaborate explanations from European systems of law which, it has to be said, have no more right to be accepted as divine truth than does the charter of the United Nations. As a piece of theology this was entirely acceptable, but the inability to distinguish between it and doctrine, between what was divinely authoritative and what was not, had serious implications. Not only did the proponents sometimes stake their lives on ideas that were not a matter of biblical inspiration, however beautifully illustrative of doctrine they were, but Scripture itself was undermined by those who were loyally dedicated to its defence.

The insistence of conservatives that the line of continuity with the past lies in the acceptance of a common corpus of doctrine has, of course, been attacked. This view, it is charged, rests on a pre-critical view of the Bible. In holding that biblical doctrine sets the limits within which theology must move, conservatives become guilty of wilful ignorance.

Conservatives have often replied, however, that a distinction needs to be made between biblical criticism as a literary device and biblical criticism as an expression of a contemporary philosophical viewpoint. The first may shed light on the text whereas the second might deny light to it. Conservatives have a critical approach to the Bible in the first sense but try not to adopt one in the second sense. What is at issue is not a matter of scholarship – conservatives holding what they do because they are unlearned and non-conservatives being unable to believe the Bible because they know too much – but a difference of world-views. The one arises from the teachings of Jesus and the apostles as recorded in Scripture and the other very often from the Enlightenment and its related developments.

This, of course, assumes that we do know what Jesus and the apostles believed; it is an assumption that has been vigorously challenged, especially by the existential theologians. The equation that conservatives make between the contents of Jesus' mind and the teachings recorded in the biblical text is dismissed with some derision. It is not unfair to say, however, that the Bultmannian attitude does not arise simply from literary considerations of the biblical text; it is a complex attitude largely informed by contemporary philosophical presuppositions. The existential theologians have undoubtedly raised provocative questions in this matter and have greatly stimulated research upon the New Testament text, but the resolution of these issues still takes place largely at the point of world-views. It is, for example, antecedently impossible for a Bultmannian to believe in the bodily resurrection of Christ because this would violate his assumption that the universe is a closed system of interlocking cause and effect; his literary work on the resurrection narratives in the Gospels, therefore, becomes a validation of this presupposition and is never the disinterested and objective piece of scholarship which it may seem to be. It is this interpretation of philosophical interests and critical concerns that has resulted in a confused situation. The fairest solution would be to say that conservatives employ the sharpest critical tools that have been developed but they do so within an acceptance of a world-view that certain other biblical scholars might think is unwise or unacceptable.

Conclusion

Conservative thought in the twentieth century has been forced to express its distinctive outlook on at least two fronts. These are sometimes quite separate and at other times are merged in one another. First, against secularism (which in the Western democracies is strongly allied to affluence but in the Marxist countries to dialectical materialism), conservative Christian faith has had to defend a supernaturalistic world-view. This defence runs the whole gamut from protecting the idea that God, in the person of the Son, has broken into our space-time world to that of arguing that the events of everyday life must be seen in the context of God's active presence in the world. Indeed, the secularist's attempt to replace God by man, to establish human pleasure as the end to which all of life's processes are made to minister, and to argue that mere human perceptions are the norms by which all things are to be judged, is the very essence of sin. What is at stake, then, is not merely the right view of salvation, but the right of Christianity to function as a world-view.

In a more limited way, conservatives have had to think hard on another front which is more explicitly religious. For it is plain that the whole, comprehensive view of salvation which the Bible presents – past, present and future, subjective and objective, personal and societal – is not being maintained in its wholeness within modern theology. Parts of the biblical doctrine have been emasculated, others diluted, still others distorted. And conservatives themselves enjoy no immunity in this respect; they, too, have to be on guard against holding less or other than what Scripture itself teaches. Yet the greater battle which has to be fought is probably less in regard to the doctrine of the Bible itself than it is in relating this to the modern world.

The matter of building bridges from Scripture into contemporary society is a complex affair that involves the whole person, for the gospel has to be set in a broader framework. The experience of salvation does not come in a vacuum. It is part of a comprehensive life-view whose termini are creation and judgment and whose substance takes in all the events of everyday life. Being saved undoubtedly means being forgiven, being spared from judgment, being renewed, indwelt and upbuilt by the Holy Spirit on the basis of Christ's finished work; but it also means assuming the mandate given to Adam to live out a life that is aesthetically satisfying, ethically significant, and socially responsible in a world that is still God's. The failure to accept the gospel ought to be seen in a broad rather than a narrow way, for it is really a refusal to live in God's world on his terms.

The preaching of the gospel is not, then, a matter simply of blitzing the air waves or of impersonally distributing tracts. Christian salvation cannot legitimately be offered when it is severed from the life-view in which it finds its context and meaning. And this framework cannot be reduced to brief slogans, isolated biblical texts or snappy bumper stickers.

The advent of modern technology and in particular mass communications has begun to work havoc, not with the biblical doctrine itself, but with the way in which it is presented. What is offered as the gospel can so easily be a depersonalized formula (guaranteed, nevertheless, to bring an experience of enduring peace and happiness) which is almost wholly disconnected from the fabric of everyday life. The new convert is then saddled with the responsibility of piecing together the fractured parts of his life and integrating these into an experience he believes is important. Sometimes he succeeds but frequently he does not.

Moreover, modern evangelism has sometimes produced an inversion of biblical priorities. In the New Testament a 'decision' for Christ is simply not countenanced apart from membership of the church. The isolation of converts from the church today − which has become the norm in some campaigns − was scarcely even imagined, let alone accepted, by the apostles. Furthermore, if a choice is to be made, one wonders whether the apostles might not have made it harder to join Jesus than the church. He himself spoke of self-crucifixion as the necessary precondition for discipleship and it is difficult to imagine a more stringent requirement.

The conservative preoccupation with doctrine and the unwillingness to wrestle with theology − that which roots doctrine in each age − is a serious problem with ramifications that lead out in many directions. It is one thing to think that one knows what the Bible says about salvation; it is quite another to know how to project this intellectually, morally, socially and evangelistically so that what the Bible actually says is not, in the process of translation, obscured, emasculated and distorted.

Notes

[1] 'A conservative is one who is marked by the desire to preserve the truth and values of the past, but his mind is not closed to change if he can be persuaded that the change is for the better': William Hordern, *New Directions in Theology Today*, I, *Introduction to Theology* (Philadelphia, 1966: London, 1968), p. 77. Hordern calls this movement 'neo-conservative' to distinguish it from the older fundamentalism. This distinction is not necessary in Britain. See George Marsden, 'Fundamentalism as an American Phenomenon: A Comparison with English Evangelicalism', *Church History*, XLVI, No. 2 (June 1977), pp. 215–232. On the American movement see E. J. Carnell, *The Case for Orthodox Theology* (Philadelphia, 1959: London, 1961), and David F. Wells and John Woodbridge, eds., *The Evangelicals: What They Believe, Who They Are, Where They are Changing* (Nashville, 1975). In this chapter, the majority of those who are 'conservative' are also evangelical; there are, nevertheless, some whose work sustains the broader evangelical movement but who themselves stand apart from it. For the period between 1890 and 1956, see Roger Nicole's fine bibliographical survey of conservative theology in Carl F. H. Henry, ed., *Contemporary Evangelical Thought* (New York, 1957), pp. 69–106. In the last two decades,

evangelicals have produced very little theology. In this chapter, then, I have assumed a role which I have not for any of the others. In the others, I have sought merely to record and assess the ideas of those under consideration; in this chapter I have actively formulated the conservative view, going beyond the role of disengaged recorder. In this chapter I have worked more as a theologian, in the others more as a historian.

[2] *Cf.* H. H. Rowley, *The Unity of the Bible* (London, 1953). See also Archibald M. Hunter, *The Unity of the New Testament* (London, 1946); George Eldon Ladd, 'Eschatology and the Unity of New Testament Theology', *Expository Times*, 68 (June 1957), pp. 268–273; Alan Richardson, 'Instrument of God; the Unity of the Biblical Doctrine of Salvation', *Interpretation*, 3 (July 1949), pp. 272–285.

[3] See Gerhard Hasel, *Old Testament Theology: Basic Issues in the Current Debate* (Grand Rapids, 1972), pp. 77–128.

[4] Lewis Sperry Chafer, *Systematic Theology*, IV (5 vols.; Dallas, 1947–48), pp. 4–52, 265–294, 313–344, 360–401.

[5] For substantiation of this view see Alva J. McClain, *The Greatness of the Kingdom* (Grand Rapids, 1959). The dispensational distinctives emerge when a comparison is made with Herman Ridderbos, *The Coming of the Kingdom* (Philadelphia, 1962). *Cf.* George Eldon Ladd, *The Presence of the Future: The Eschatology of Biblical Realism* (Grand Rapids, 1974) = *Jesus and the Kingdom* (London, 1966).

[6] O. T. Allis, 'Dispensationalism and the Doctrine of the Unity of Scripture', *Evangelical Quarterly*, 8, No. 1 (January 1936), pp. 22–35. This contention is sustained by Daniel P. Fuller. See, for example, his discussion on the Abrahamic covenant in *The Hermeneutics of Dispensationalism* (Chicago, 1957), pp. 214–231. Ryrie has either modified this older dispensationalism or at least accented features in it such as the pervasiveness of grace in all the dispensations, which brings it closer to covenant theology. See his *Dispensationalism Today* (Chicago, 1965), pp. 110–131.

[7] John Murray, *The Covenant of Grace* (London, 1953); 'Covenant', *The New Bible Dictionary*, pp. 264–268. *Cf.* Ernest F. Kevan, 'The Covenants and the Interpretation of the Old Testament', *Evangelical Quarterly*, 26, No. 1 (January 1956), pp. 19–28; Meredith Kline, 'Law Covenant', *Westminster Theological Journal*, 27, No. 1 (1964), pp. 1–20; Leon Morris, *The Apostolic Preaching of the Cross* (London, 1964: Grand Rapids, 1965), pp. 65–111; Geerhardus Vos, *Biblical Theology: Old and New Testaments* (Grand Rapids, 1948), pp. 52–202.

[8] J. Barton Payne, *The Theology of the Older Testament* (Grand Rapids, 1962), p. 241. See also Geoffrey W. Grogan, 'The Experience of Salvation in the Old and New Testaments', *Vox Evangelica*, V (1967), pp. 4–26.

[9] R. K. Harrison, *Introduction to the Old Testament* (Grand Rapids, 1969: London, 1970), p.479. The idea of the covenant in its theological aspect, which is sustained by these and other contemporary authors, coincides precisely with what many older authors affirmed. (See, *e.g.*, A. B. Davidson, *The Theology of the Old Testament* [Edinburgh, 1911], pp. 235–289). What is new is the more precise and extended knowledge of the role of covenants in the ancient Near Eastern life. This is critically examined by Meredith G. Kline, *Treaty of the Great King: The Covenant Structure of Deuteronomy* (Grand Rapids, 1963). Indeed, this new knowledge has served only to point up the authenticity of the Old Testament records. 'It is becoming increasingly evident', says Kenneth Kitchen, 'that – regardless of the date of the forms – the literary characteristics of the Ancient Near Eastern treaties make nonsense of the usual criteria of conventional literary criticism.' *Ancient Orient and Old Testament* (Chicago and London, 1966), p. 101, n. 52.

[10] Francis Foulkes, *The Acts of God: A Study of the Basis of Typology in the Old Testament* (London, 1958), Walter Kaiser, *Toward an Old Testament Theology* (Grand Rapids, 1978); F. F. Bruce, *This is That: The New Testament Development of some Old Testament Themes* (Grand Rapids, 1968 [as *New Testament Development of Old Testament Themes*]: Exeter, 1969); 'Promise and

Fulfillment in Paul's Presentation of Jesus', *Promise and Fulfillment,* ed. F. F. Bruce (Edinburgh, 1963). *Cf.* R. V. G. Tasker, *The Old Testament in the New Testament* (Grand Rapids, 1963).

[11] *Cf.* F. F. Bruce, 'Our God and Saviour', *The Saviour God,* ed. S. G. F. Brandon (Manchester, 1963); Richard N. Longenecker, *The Christology of Early Jewish Christianity* (London, 1970), pp. 39–41.

[12] *E.g.* John F. Sawyer, *Semantics in Biblical Research: New Methods in Defining Hebrew Words for Salvation* (London, 1972).

[13] See E. M. B. Green, *The Meaning of Salvation* (London and Philadelphia, 1965), pp. 11–54 and 96–118; Ronald Ward, *Royal Theology: Our Lord's Teaching About God* (London, 1964), pp. 151–210.

[14] I. Howard Marshall, *The Origins of New Testament Christology* (Leicester and Downers Grove, 1976), pp. 63–82; Richard N. Longenecker, ' "Son of Man" as a Self-Description of Jesus', *Journal of the Evangelical Theological Society*, 12, No. 3 (Summer, 1969), pp. 151–158; ' "Son of Man" Imagery: Some Implications for Theology and Discipleship', *Journal of the Evangelical Theological Society*, 18, No. 1 (Winter, 1975), pp. 3–16.

[15] 'It comes as something of a surprise, for example, to find that, apart from the crucifixion narrative and one verse in Hebrews, Paul is the only New Testament writer to speak about "the cross".' Leon Morris, *The Cross in the New Testament* (Exeter and Grand Rapids, 1965), pp. 216–217. Paul, however, is not at odds with the other authors on this theme, as Morris shows, and as Joachim Jeremias in his *The Central Message of the New Testament* (London and New York, 1965), argues.

[16] Herman Ridderbos, *Paul and Jesus: Origin and General Character of Paul's Preaching of Christ* (Philadelphia, 1958); F. F. Bruce, *Paul and Jesus* (Grand Rapids, 1974: London, 1977); Archibald M. Hunter, *Paul and his Predecessors* (London and Philadelphia, 1961); J. W. Fraser, *Jesus and Paul: Paul as Interpreter of Jesus from Harnack to Kümmel* (Abingdon, 1976).

[17] Green, pp. 152–189.

[18] Omitted for reasons of space is any discussion on adjunct doctrines such as 'calling,' 'adoption,' 'conversion' and 'regeneration'. See John Murray, *Redemption Accomplished and Applied* (Grand Rapids, 1955), pp. 88–116, 132–140; Robert Knudsen, 'The Nature of Regeneration', *Christian Faith and Modern Theology,* pp. 305–322.

[19] G. Kittel and G. Friedrich, eds., *Theological Dictionary of the New Testament* (Grand Rapids, 1964–74), VII, pp. 992–994.

[20] Morris, *The Apostolic Preaching of the Cross,* pp. 11–64; 'Redeemer', 'Redemption', *The New Bible Dictionary,* pp. 1078, 1079. See also I. Howard Marshall, 'The Development of the Concept of Redemption in the New Testament', *Reconciliation and Hope: New Testament Essays on Atonement and Eschatology,* ed. Robert Banks (Exeter and Grand Rapids, 1974), pp. 153–172.

[21] There is a peculiar identity that is struck in many negro spirituals between black suffering and Christ's, their captivity and his humiliation, their hope for release and his resurrection from the dead. It was an identity interpreted spiritually, not politically: 'I'm a chile of God wid my soul set free, / For Christ hab bought my liberty.' There was an intense yearning that Jesus would do for them what he had done for others, such as feed them, protect them and save them. See James H. Cone, *The Spirituals and the Blues: An Interpretation* (New York, 1972).

[22] Morris, *The Apostolic Preaching of the Cross,* pp. 214–250. Herman Ridderbos, *Paul: An Outline of his Theology* (Grand Rapids, 1975: London, 1977), pp. 182–205; Ralph P. Martin, 'Reconciliation and Forgiveness in Colossians', *Reconciliation and Hope,* pp. 104–124; John Murray, 'The Reconciliation', *Westminster Theological Journal,* 29 (1966–67), pp. 1–23.

[23] Morris, *The Apostolic Preaching of the Cross,* pp. 144–213. The argument is developed against the view summed up by Richardson who admits that the word *propitiation* appears four times in the RV but perversely claims that 'it is time to say that propitiation in the usual meaning of the word is hardly a biblical idea at all. . . . The idea of placating an irascible deity is almost

totally absent from the Bible, although it forms a large part of pagan religion and cults.' Alan Richardson, *An Introduction to the Theology of the New Testament* (London and New York, 1958), p. 223. See J. Clement Connell, 'The Propitiation Element in the Atonement', *Vox Evangelica*, IV (1965), pp. 28–42. Roger R. Nicole, 'C. H. Dodd and the Doctrine of Propitiation', *Westminster Theological Journal*, 17 (1955), pp. 117–157. On the means of propitiation, the 'blood' of Christ, see A. M. Stibbs, *The Meaning of the Word 'Blood' in Scripture* (London, 1947) who counters the ideas of Vincent Taylor, especially in his *The Atonement in New Testament Teaching* and *Jesus and His Sacrifice*, that 'blood' stands, not for Jesus' death, but for his life which is released from the body to serve other purposes (such as imbuing the sacraments with significance).

[24] See, for example, Samuel Mikolaski, 'P. T. Forsyth on the Atonement', *Evangelical Quarterly*, 36 (January–March 1964), pp. 27–41; (April–June, 1964), pp. 78–91; 'Principal James Denney on the Atonement', *Evangelical Quarterly*, 35 (April–June 1963), pp.89–96; (July–September 1963), pp. 144–148; (October–December 1963), pp. 209–222; 'R. W. Dale on the Atonement', *Evangelical Quarterly*, 35 (January–March 1963), pp. 23–29.

[25] See Leon Morris, *The Wages of Sin: An Examination of the New Testament Teaching on Death* (London, 1954); Leon Morris, *The Biblical Doctrine of Judgment* (London, 1960); R. V. G. Tasker, *The Biblical Doctrine of the Wrath of God* (London, 1971).

[26] Justification was treated biblically by Morris, Tasker and Bruce, and historically by Bromiley, Parker, Packer, Hughes, Bolster and Stibbs in *The Evangelical Quarterly*, volumes for January, April and July, 1952. See also Lorman Petersen, 'The Nature of Justification', *Christian Faith and Modern Theology*, pp 347–370; Carl F. H. Henry, 'Justification by Ignorance: A Neo-Protestant Motif', *Journal of the Evangelical Theological Society*, 13, No. 1 (Winter, 1970), pp. 3–14; George Eldon Ladd, *A Theology of the New Testament* (Grand Rapids, 1974: London, 1975), pp. 437–456.

[27] Wolfhart Pannenberg, *Jesus – God and Man* (London and Philadelphia, 1968), pp. 258–268. The insistence on substitution is developed against those who see Jesus merely as 'representative', standing in man's place doing what man cannot do for himself, as in G. W. H. Lampe, *Reconciliation in Christ*, and Vincent Taylor's *The Atonement in New Testament Teaching*. The notion is not so much wrong as incomplete, for Jesus could not represent men without substituting for them, as James D. G. Dunn in effect argues, despite his misgivings over the latter word. (See his essay 'Paul's Understanding of the Death of Jesus', *Reconciliation and Hope*, pp. 125–141). The crux of the argument, Ladd sums up, is whether or not the atonement 'is wrought entirely outside of and apart from ourselves so that we have nothing to do but accept its benefits' (*A Theology of the New Testament*, p. 428); if this is the case, as he believes the apostles taught, then we should secure its truth by using the word *substitutionary*. For a brief summary of the issues and biblical evidence see E. Brandenburger, 'Cross', *The New International Dictionary of New Testament Theology*, ed. Colin Brown (Exeter and Grand Rapids, 1975), I, pp. 394–403.

[28] The charge made by Catholics that this view represents 'extrincism' stems from misunderstanding. The pardon of justification is never divorced in conservative theology from the ideas of faith and union with Christ. It is not merely a legal decision handed down from the judge, but it is the means of identification with Christ. *Cf.* Louis Bouyer, *The Spirit and Forms of Protestantism* (London, 1956: Westminster, 1961), pp. 136–165.

[29] James I. Packer, 'What did the Cross Achieve? The Logic of Penal Substitution', *Tyndale Bulletin*, 25 (1974), pp. 1–13.

[30] *Cf.* Arthur F. Holmes, 'Three Levels of Meaning in God-Language', *Journal of the Evangelical Theological Society*, 16, No. 2 (Winter 1973), pp. 83–94, and his essay 'Language, Logic and Faith', in *Jerusalem and Athens*, ed. E. R. Geehan (Grand Rapids, 1971).

[31] The most substantial defence of the penal motif in the atonement is in Emil Brunner, *The Mediator: A Study of the Central Doctrine of the Christian Faith* (London, 1934: Philadelphia, 1947), pp. 455–536; the most common objection is that the penal motif which is 'not a

legitimate child of biblical revelation' arises 'from the imputation to God of attitudes and modes of behaviour on which the Bible stands in judgment'. It produces a set of relations which are 'superficial' and 'artificial' and lacking the personal element. H. A. Hodges, *The Pattern of Atonement* (London, 1955), pp. 43–49.

[32] Gustav Aulén, *Christus Victor, An Historical Study of the Three Main Types of the Idea of Atonement* (London, 1931: New York, 1954), pp. 143–160.

[33] Tertullian, *De Poen.*, 7, 6.

[34] Tertullian, *De Poen.*, 9, 2.

[35] John Wesley's own book, *A Plain Account of Christian Perfection* (London, 1968), is a record of his thought on this subject over a fifty year period. Probably the most illuminating single passage elsewhere appears in a sermon where he declares: 'Although we may, "by the Spirit, mortify the deeds of the body," resist and conquer both outward and inward sin: although we may *weaken* our enemies day by day; yet we cannot *drive them out*. By all the grace which is given at justification we cannot extirpate them. Though we watch and pray ever so much, we cannot wholly cleanse either our hearts or hands. Most sure we cannot till it shall please our Lord to speak to our hearts again, to speak the second time, "Be clean"; and then only the leprosy is cleansed. Then only, the evil root, the carnal mind, is destroyed; and inbred sin subsists no more. But if there be no such second change, if there be no instantaneous deliverance after justification, if there be *none but* a gradual work of God (that there is a gradual work none denies), then we must be content, as well as we can, to remain full of sin till death.' John Wesley, *The Standard Sermons of John Wesley*, ed. E. H. Sugden (London, 1951), II, pp. 340–391. *Cf.* I. Howard Marshall, 'Sanctification in the Teaching of John Wesley and John Calvin', *Evangelical Quarterly*, 34, No. 2 (April–June 1962), pp. 75–82. The Wesleyan approach is excellently set forth in Mildred Wynkoop, *A Theology of Love: The Dynamic of Wesleyanism* (Kansas City, 1972).

[36] Louis Berkhof, *Systematic Theology* (London, 1959), p. 533.

[37] On Pentecostalism, see Nils Block-Hoell, *The Pentecostal Movement* (London, 1964); on charismatics, Richard Quebedeaux, *The New Charismatics: The Origins, Development, and Significance of Neo-Pentecostalism* (New York, 1976). The double experiences in question are those recorded in Acts 2:33; 4:31; 8:17; 9:17; 10:44; 19:6. On this matter see James D. Dunn, *Baptism in the Holy Spirit* (London and Napierville, 1970), Frederick Dale Bruner, *A Theology of The Holy Spirit* (Grand Rapids, 1970: London, 1971), and John R. W. Stott, *Baptism and Fullness* (London and Downers Grove, 1975).

[38] Geerhardus Vos, *The Pauline Eschatology* (Grand Rapids, 1961), and Clark H. Pinnock, 'The Structure of Pauline Eschatology', *Evangelical Quarterly*, 37 (1965), pp. 9–20; G. C. Berkouwer, *The Return of Christ* (Grand Rapids, 1971); G. R. Beasley-Murray, *Jesus and the Future* (London, 1954). Differences in eschatological conviction emerged clearly at the 1971 Jerusalem Prophecy Conference. Carl F. H. Henry, ed., *Prophecy in the Making* (Carol Stream, 1971). For a succinct summary of the basic differences, see Robert G. Clouse, ed., *The Meaning of the Millennium: Four Views* (Downers Grove, 1977).

[39] *Cf.* G. C. Berkouwer, *Faith and Perseverance* (Grand Rapids, 1958) and I. Howard Marshall, *Kept by the Power of God: A Study of Perseverance and Falling Away* (London, 1969: Minneapolis, 1975), for the two opposing views.

[40] Abraham Kuyper, *Lectures on Calvinism* (Grand Rapids, 1970), pp. 9–170; the same outlook is expressed by Emil Brunner. The question of work is dealt with in his *Christianity and Civilization* (2 vols; London, 1949), I, pp. 57–71.

[41] J. N. D. Anderson, *Into the World: The Need and Limits of Christian Involvement* (London, 1968); *Morality, Law and Grace* (London, 1972).

[42] Philip Watson, 'Luther's Doctrine of Vocation', *Scottish Journal of Theology*, II, No. 4 (1949), pp. 364–377; Gustav Wingren, *Luther on Vocation* (Philadelphia, 1957); O. C. A.

Rupprecht, 'Remedy for Modern Chaos – Luther's Concept of Our Calling', *Concordia Theological Monthly*, II (1951), pp. 820–847.

[43] See John R. W. Stott, *The Lausanne Covenant: An Exposition and Commentary* (London and Minneapolis, 1975), pp. 25–29; John R. W. Stott, 'The Significance of Lausanne', *International Review of Missions*, 64, No. 255 (July 1975), pp. 288–294.

[44] This is the thesis of John R. W. Stott's *Christian Mission in the Modern World* (London, 1975).

[45] The social record is reviewed reasonably well in John Wesley Bready, *England: Before and After Wesley* (London, 1938). See also Leonard Elliott-Binns, *The Early Evangelicals: A Religious and Social Study* (London, 1953). These studies need to be put in the general context provided by J. H. Whitely, *Wesley's England: A Survey of XVIIIth Century Social and Cultural Conditions* (London, 1938). Relatively little work has been done specifically on John Wesley in this regard, but see Maldwyn Edwards, *John Wesley and the Eighteenth Century: A Study of his Social and Political Influence* (London, 1933). More recently fresh studies have been produced on the members of the so-called Clapham Sect such as David Newsome's *The Wilberforces and Henry Manning: The Parting of Friends* (Cambridge, Mass., 1966) and the brief biography by G. F. A. Best entitled *Shaftesbury* (London, 1964).

[46] See Richard V. Pierard, 'Social Concern in Christian Missions', *Christianity Today*, XX, No. 19 (18 June 1976), pp. 7–10. Pierard argues that many missionaries 'stood for social justice, fought against inhuman practices in traditional societies, and resisted the worst features of advancing European imperialism'. In evidence, he cites general studies such as James S. Dennis' three-volumed work, *Christian Missions and Social Progress,* regional studies like Kenneth Ingham's *Reformers in India, 1793–1833* and individual case studies as exemplified by John Philip whose own study, *Researches in South Africa*, so deeply influenced opinion in Britain on South Africa.

The 'dialectic theologians' may well jot down their dogmatics on a scrap of paper: God is not man, revelation and redemption are not history, eternity is not time. Whatever else they may have to say, can only be a repetition of these sentences.

Wilhelm Schmidt

Barth has the ability, to a very large degree, of being able to employ the language of Scripture in a system that is totally foreign to the Bible.

Gustav Wingren

I was and I am a common or garden theologian.

Karl Barth

Chapter Two

Neo-orthodoxy

European theology reached one of its dramatic turning points shortly after the First World War. In North America it came a decade later. On both sides of the Atlantic the kingdom of God had been equated with social progress by the Protestant liberals; on both sides this equation was shattered, in the one case by war and in the other by the Great Depression. The familiar propositions of man's innate goodness and God's untroubled benevolence could no longer be squared with reality. Not only were cities and lives destroyed but so was the naive theology of the liberals.

The theological reaction, spearheaded by Karl Barth, itself soon bifurcated into two 'schools' often antagonistic to one another. The division was complete by the early 1930s. Barth and Brunner, supported shortly afterwards by the Scandinavians, Nygren and Aulén, roughly constituted one emphasis. Tillich, Bultmann, and the Niebuhrs constituted the other.[1] As sharp as their internal differences have been, however, it needs to be remembered that they have all shared a common rejection of classical liberalism and all owe a common debt to Søren Kierkegaard.

It is by no means a simple task summarizing the conclusions reached by either of these two schools on the matter of salvation. If there are shared emphases, there are also pointed differences. There are differences, for example, in output, the colossal and intimidating edifice of Barth's thought not being matched either in size or in complexity by any of the other theologians classified here as neo-orthodox; there are differences of tradition, Nygren and Aulén being Lutheran, Barth and Brunner being Reformed; there are differences of approach, Nygren and Aulén utilizing history as part of their theological methodology, while Barth and Brunner are more purely theological and Cullmann more obviously exegetical; finally, there are the obvious differences of opinion which have been pursued vigorously.

The grouping of these theologians into one 'school', then, is an artificial device, yet it is not without its benefits in spite of the obvious drawbacks.

Is there a common core of ideas to which each of those here classified as neo-orthodox would assent? Is it possible to find this agreement in spite of the different ways in which it is formulated and the different theological contexts in which it is fashioned? The agreement may only be rudimentary, but it can certainly be found in these three propositions: first, it is God who saves; second, he saves in Christ in whom he conquers man's enemies; third, the traditional doctrines of justification, conversion, sanctification, faith and judgment are all in need of restatement.

The divine initiative

First, then, it is *God* who saves. The simplest and most effective statement of this is to be found in Nygren's *Agape and Eros*. In this work, Nygren distinguishes between two different religious loves, *agapē* and *erōs*, and shows how they have either been confused or, far less commonly, differentiated in the church's long history.[2]

Erōs is self-love, self-justifying, self-seeking love. *Agapē* is self-giving, self-sacrificing, self-abnegating love. The first is the sinner's love; the second is God's love.[3]

Erōs loves out of a profit-and-loss mentality. It seeks its object, not spontaneously, but because it calculates that it is in its interest to do so. With respect to God, this kind of love is simply an extension of ordinary, human love, having at its centre need and want and being driven by the will to get and possess. More precisely, it is driven by the desire to possess God. It attempts to do this by immortalizing itself and forcing him into obligation to it. Salvation is therefore seen as its own work, its upward way to God, that by which it grasps him out of need and acquisitive desire.

Erōs, then, recognizes the value of God for man and wants him for that reason but *agapē* love is quite different. The former recognizes the worth of its object; the latter creates value in its object which is man. It gives itself to its object in uncalculating spontaneity. It gives itself away sacrificially. *Agapē* is God's love, God's way of salvation, God himself reaching down to man. The Christian idea of salvation, then, begins with God, not with man, and abolishes every effort at self-justification. Elsewhere Nygren has contrasted the 'common' and the Christian views of atonement thus:

> Over against this the Christian view of atonement stands for the complete abolition of the common idea of atonement. No fellowship with God without atonement — that is true; only, atonement is not a work of man, but of God Himself. No atonement without sacrifice — this principle, too, retains its validity in Christianity; only, it is not man who offers the sacrifice and not God who accepts it, but it is God who sacrifices Himself in Christ. Christianity is not the demand for an atonement and reconciliation which man must effect so as to open the way for himself to fellowship with God. Christianity is the word of reconciliation, the message of how God has made a way for Himself to us so as to bring us into fellowship with Himself.[4]

Likewise, Aulén sees the essence of salvation to be in the initiative taken by the *agapē* – God[5] confronting the enemies and powers of darkness who oppress men. So great are these enemies — the law, wrath, sin, death, the devil — that self-salvation is simply ridiculous. There is, he says, 'no way from man to God, no way in which man could gradually strive upward toward the divine. The way to fellowship with God is God's way to man.'[6]

The presupposition of this view of salvation is the relationship in which God and man are placed, and here we touch the heart of the Lundensian theology. Man is a sinner, a rebel, spontaneously and persistently evil, guilty before God, bound by wrath, captured by the devil. He is worthless and hopeless outside of God's saving *agapē*. 'God is God and man is his religious contradiction,'[7] is the way Ferré sums up their view.

It is no secret, of course, that Barth and in slightly different ways Brunner and Cullmann have done much to establish this same emphasis in the face of the older liberalism. In a perceptive if scathing essay, Gustav Wingren has suggested that the controlling *Geist* of Barth's theology is not so much its creative restatement of Reformation ideas, but its reactionary inversion of the liberal view. There man was the focus; here God is. There God was immersed in man; here God is excluded from the world with the single exception of the

55

intrusion of the Word in the God-man. At best, only a shadow of the divine is ever seen to cross the surface of human life. 'Everything the Bible says', Wingren argues, 'is incorporated within this Platonic frame of reference which is never broken.'[8] The result, however, is that Barth, for his own reasons, extolls the free, sovereign grace of God as vigorously and voluminously as anyone. 'Man', he declares in one place, 'is not in a position to atone for his transgression, to reconcile himself to God. Man cannot bring forth a Jesus Christ in which his atonement with God can take place. If it is to take place,' he continues, 'it must be from God, in the freedom of God and not of man, in the freedom of the grace of God, to which we have no claim, which would necessarily judge and condemn us, because we have sinned against it and always will sin against it, because we have shown ourselves unworthy of it.'[9] To this affirmation, strings of others could be added.

The reasons for affirming human inability are, of course, well known and led Barth into a vigorous debate with Brunner.[10] Barth vehemently rejected any possibility of a natural or 'twilight' knowledge of God left behind as a residue after the 'fall'.[11] There is no latent perception of God upon which salvation-knowledge builds. The destruction of the *imago Dei* consequent upon the 'fall' means, not merely that man is shut out from fellowship with God, but that he is also totally devoid of the means and the desire to approach God.

From the divine aspect, Barth's conviction about the indispensability of God's initiative is given theological form in the idea of covenant. The doctrine of reconciliation which, for Barth, includes the doctrines of sin, justification, sanctification and the church, is simply the concrete outworking of a covenant established by God in eternity with man. This covenant is the presupposition of reconciliation and reconciliation is the fulfilment of covenant.[12]

In conservative theology, covenant was defined as God's initiative in establishing a saving relationship with men, beginning with Noah and ending with the church. This covenant was made known after the fall and it has set up a line of demarcation between those who, being elect, know God (or, in Arminian theology, know God and therefore are elect) and those who do not and are lost.

Barth agrees that the covenant is not a two-sided contract but, rather, is an expression of divine monergism. There is, however, only one covenant which has different moments of expression – Noah, Moses, Abraham – and its objects are not so much individual people as the whole human race. Thus, the covenant is God's eternal purpose to take man into fellowship with himself which antedates the creation; indeed, the creation and, in a sense, man's 'fall' are the means to its realization. It pre-eminently concerns Jesus Christ in whom man stands and on whom alone the decrees of election and reprobation have their terminus.[13] It is Christ, not individual men, who is elect (and they are elect in him), and he is reprobate (and reprobate because of them). Because of God's purpose to take humanity to himself through Christ it is appropriate, Barth says, to speak of the 'humanity of God'.[14]

The novel features in this formulation emerge in Barth's threefold criticism of conservative theology.[15] First, he charges the old 'federal' theologians with 'historicizing' the biblical message, because fellowship with God was established through the Old Testament covenants on a basis other than Christ's work and word; second, they 'rationalized' it, distinguishing between a covenant of works (the conditions God established with Adam for the perseverance of the divine-human fellowship) and the covenant of grace (the means taken by God to redeem man from his rebellion and save him from destruction); third, they 'psychologized' it, seeing its outworking in doctrines of personal election and reprobation.

There are, in comparison with the other neo-orthodox scholars, peculiarities in Barth's articulation of divine monergism. If Brunner is agreed that Adam was not an historical figure, he and others are in sharp disagreement that sin has destroyed the *imago Dei,* for that would leave man no more responsible for his rebellion than a stock or a stone. What distinguishes man from the animals is the existence of this *imago*, and its loss would mean the disappearance of man as something different from and elevated above the mere animal world. The *imago*, furthermore would be 'a purely archaeological fact', as John Baillie puts it, and our knowledge of it should only be by historical research. In fact, we know about it because we desire knowledge of it from ourselves directly, and Baillie goes on to affirm that the presence of rationality, an ability to distinguish right from wrong, and a sense of something awesome and holy in the midst of life, are the indispensable prerequisites for successful preaching of the gospel. For Barth, the 'gospel necessitates a completely new nature, miraculously conceived, since there is nothing within man which it can supplement or change'; the preacher, counters Baillie, 'is indeed calling upon God to perform a miracle, but not *that* miracle – and not that miracle precisely for the reason that he is also calling upon *man* to do something, namely, to decide for God'.[16] There is no agreement, then, that Barth is correct in his extreme christocentrism, by which not only salvation but also revelation alone comes through Christ, and in Christ alone the decrees of election and rebrobation have their terminus; nor is there agreement that his novel interpretation of covenant is valid. Yet there is full agreement that it is *God* who saves, that he saves because he alone has the power, wisdom and love to do it, and that any thought of man being able to work his way upward to God is a violation of the whole Christian message.

The christological focus

The distinction between *christo*logical and *theo*logical concerns which may be suggested by this treatment is, of course, entirely foreign to Barth.[17] It is God who meets us in Christ. When our theology centres on Christ it necessarily centres on God; when we speak of Christ's work on the cross, we are necessarily speaking of God's work on the cross. The transition from our first general proposition to the second is therefore very easy and the only question which it raises, especially from the Barthian perspective, is whether the correct order is not here reversed. The second proposition, however, is that God saves in Christ in whom he conquers man's enemies and man's 'fallen' nature.

The most direct statement of this comes from the Lundensians, especially Aulén, and its most complex and prolix form is found in Barth. Aulén and Nygren articulate this theme in terms of the classic motif of atonement, constantly opposing it to the penal or Latin theory which they reject. On the other hand, Barth, while reiterating Aulén's *Christus Victor* theme, seeks to integrate penal motifs with it. Brunner makes the penal motif his starting point, and the classic idea is given but a minor place in an integrated whole. There are, therefore, differences between these theologians, both as to how the classic theory should be stated and how much of it should be utilized in trying to understand Christ's work.

Aulén's study *Christus Victor,* in which this thought is developed, is, like Nygren's *Agape and Eros,* both a theological thesis and an attempted historical validation of it. The thesis is that at the cross the *agapē*-God gave himself to man by destroying man's enemies, law, wrath, sin, death and the devil.[18] The cross was the occasion when the world of evil was overcome and destroyed by God. This, Aulén says, is what the New Testament declares and what Luther recovered; his historical efforts attempt to show how, in the intervening period as well as the one which followed Luther, this idea was lost or distorted.

The conflict at the cross does not take place within God himself, one part of him bearing man's sin and the other withdrawing in horror; still less does it involve a trinitarian disjuncture between the Father who sacrifices and the Son who is sacrificed. These are the ambiguities, even crudities, that have been injected into discussions on the atonement by the proponents of the Latin theory. The conflict is not even primarily ethical at base, good confronting evil. It is personal, God overwhelming the devil.[19] When Aulén speaks of God's wrath, then, it is always in this context. 'The wrath of God', Ferré says in summary, 'is the intensity with which the love of God affirms its own purity',[20] but it is affirmed over against the world of supernatural wickedness. As such there were in Jesus' life anticipations of the final conflict at the cross, for throughout his life he was buffeted by the devil and repulsed him. He did in his death, then, what he did not do in his life only in the sense of conquering the devil *finally,* for previously Jesus had temporarily rebuffed him. Undoubtedly, as Aulén claims, the incarnation and atonement are here made continuous with one another in a way that becomes impossible when penal motifs are allowed to influence the discussion.[21] To say that they are continuous, however, is simply another way of denying to the death of Christ elements not present in his life.

The theology of Barth is so complex and many-sided, and those struggling to find their way through its ordered prolixities so frequently discover unexpected themes and word relationships, that a great deal of diversity is found among his interpreters. It has, for example, been customary to view Barth as a cautious, modified proponent of the Latin theory. There is certainly evidence of this kind of thought in his *Church Dogmatics* especially in the section on the atonement.[22] When the atonement is placed in the broader context of his theology, however, it is probably more accurate to speak of him as being primarily an exponent of the classic motif as Donald Bloesch has suggested.[23] There is broad agreement that both themes are present in Barth; the differences are over which motif is dominant.

Salvation in Barth's thought is in three quite distinct stages: creation, reconciliation and redemption, the last being largely future and eschatological. To see creation as the first act of salvation and to speak of it as a token of grace as he does is, of course, a reinterpretation of supralapsarianism. His thought is that the darkness which was overcome by light in Genesis 1 was a metaphysical force. It is, in his parlance, chaos *(das Nichtige)* or Nothingness, which is not quite equivalent to the usual meaning of the word *evil* in conservative thought. By chaos, Barth does not mean a force of active opposition to God which has an existence of its own and a personal centre in the devil. He does not believe in the devil at all and thinks of this chaos as privation, the absence of good, something which is powerful but which has no life of its own. This chaos had to be overthrown if the covenant plan was to be put into effect with the creation of man and then his redemption.

In the second stage, this power has to be destroyed, for as non-being it threatens all of life and man himself. Jesus confronted it throughout his life, but supremely at the cross where it was destroyed.[24] This does not mean that 'evil' has ceased to exist; it still exists in the sense that it has power over men's minds. It has the same power that any illusion has which, as long as it is believed and to the extent to which it is believed, can control a person's life.

At the same time, there is a penal motif present in Barth. He affirms the idea that Jesus stood in man's place, doing for man what man could never do for himself. He denies, however, that this either changes the attitude of God toward man or that it happens outside of man and then, through the Spirit, is applied to him. Rather, by identification man himself died in Christ and ceased to exist. Golgotha, he states bluntly, was the end of the world. Sinners there disappeared and apostate mankind terminated its life. The word used by Barth to describe this is *Versöhnung,* which Bromiley has regularly translated as 'atonement' rather than 'reconciliation'. If this is correct, then it needs to be said that something other than a traditional utilization of penal and substitutionary ideas is in view. If suffering is necessitated by this act of reconciliation, it is only as an accompaniment to the act rather than as an integral part of it. Barth is not thinking of Christ standing in the sinner's stead, absorbing his punishment and, through the Spirit, freeing man to appropriate this by faith. The element of appropriation is almost overlooked by Barth, and the objective side, humanity hearing the divine Yes through Christ, is so overplayed that he is obliged to give a convoluted and qualified affirmation to universalism. This, naturally, is the third and final stage of salvation.

The relation between classic and penal motifs is handled rather more satisfactorily by Brunner. In his treatment of redemption, which is but one of several salvation-words he employs, he sees a natural articulation with the classic motif.[25] The biblical way of understanding the atonement, he insists, is not primarily and certainly not exclusively in this direction, but rather through the ideas of legal debt and guilt which require the shedding of blood. These are ideas which 'have become wholly alien to the thought of the present day'.[26] They have become strange and offensive to us, not because in our enlightenment we have advanced beyond them, but because we have become unaccustomed to thinking in terms of special revelation.

Undoubtedly the penal motif, when crystallized into a logical theorem, is vulnerable to criticism, for it is by no means clear how precisely sin and righteousness are exchanged between the sinner and Christ, whether Christ's suffering is itself the punishment or merely the indication of punishment taking place, and how divine wrath is actually assuaged. Yet Brunner, with unswerving fidelity to Scripture at this point, insists on speaking its language and thus seeing forensic ideas as alone able to do justice to both the full nature of God and the profundity of justification through Christ. He repudiates 'the modern, unilateral, monistic Idea of God'[27] who is bare *agapē,* in favour of the biblical notion of him who is both *agapē* and *nomos,* both love and holiness, both hidden and revealed, merciful and yet whose anger is real and objective and in the face of which and outside of Christ man is in deathly peril.[28] This type of dualism in the nature of God, often expressed in language drawn from Luther and which Brunner calls a 'dialectic', is seldom more than the affirmation of that kind of mystery which alone protects the seriousness of the forensic cast of the biblical material. And the tight integration which Brunner achieves between the person and the work of Christ makes futile the charge that proponents of the penal motif must depersonalize God's relations with men. The very reverse is the truth. To be the object of God's wrath is not merely to be the recipient of an unfavourable ruling by a dispassionate judge. It is to be confronted by God *himself,* by God whose holiness is kindled against all that defiles what he has made. This divine and objective reality, this awesome wrath, stands poised against all of those who have not found safety in the propitiation of Jesus where love has broken through this wrath. In his articulation of these themes, Brunner has placed himself strangely out of step with much of neo-orthodoxy but has rendered the great service of insisting that Scripture be read and taken seriously when it utilizes this kind of language in explaining Christ's work on the cross.

Reinterpreting biblical themes

The third general proposition on which there is agreement is in the argument that the traditional doctrines of justification, conversion, sanctification, faith and judgment are in need of modification. The modifications sought, however, have all been in different directions. The Lutherans, ever wary of the penal element, have worked out these doctrines in terms of *agapē*; Barth, increasingly alarmed by the direction in which Bultmann was taking theology, almost outlawed any subjective aspect in favour of the objective, and Brunner, more fascinated by the thought of personal encounter, has written into his theology more existential notions.[29]

The classic motif, dominating the thought of Aulén and Nygren, plainly controls how these other doctrines are constructed. In short, the Christian life is about Christ's conquest over man's enemies. With Aulén, the subjective aspect of this is rather vague. Justification is 'simply the atonement brought into the present',[30] but sanctification is seen as an aspect of justification.[31] This is a precautionary move against those who might argue that God justifies a person on the grounds of what he sees the man will become. The spectre of a works doctrine forces Aulén to condense 'conditional' sanctification into 'positional', to see this as a part of justification. Justification is then itself truncated by being made synonomous with the forgiveness of sins.[32] Although he speaks of salvation being in the present tense he is opposed to any concentration on inward piety and is content, instead, for Christians to love their neighbours and find their calling.

Both Aulén and Nygren eliminate the penal aspect from justification. Although the former uses penal language such as 'imputed' and 'declared' righteousness, he denies that this means the remission of punishment; rather it is, he says, the restoration of a filial relationship. Likewise Nygren, in his comments on Romans 3:25, is obliged to translate *hilastērion* as 'mercy seat', but he insists that this does not mean that the love and the justice of God were opposed to one another and that in Christ's cross they found their resolution. There is little thought of God's obligation to uphold the law in his relation with sinners; rather, God's righteousness is his destructive goodness against man's enemies. Justification is entering into this destruction. On the other hand, Nygren is more satisfactory in his understanding of the present, experiential aspect of salvation. As one would expect, there is a strong sacramental emphasis in both theologians. Nygren unites 1 Corinthians 12:3, referring to Spirit baptism, with Romans 6:3, a text on water baptism, and thereby argues for baptismal regeneration. Yet it is the Word, in both sacraments, which is efficacious. 'The formula "justification by faith alone" ', Aulén sums up, 'is a statement about that continuing redemptive activity which *the living Christ present and active* in the Word and the sacraments carries on in and through his Church.'[33] This approach represents a substantial blurring of the doctrines as conceived traditionally.

Traditionally, the *ordo salutis* has been presented in a series of steps – calling, regeneration, illumination, justification, conversion, sanctification, glorification – but for Barth, this chain of thought is full of 'uncertainties, contradictions and exegetical and conceptual arbitrariness and artificiality'.[34] He argues instead for one divine act which simply has different moments. This certainly leads to a rejection of the distinction between objective and subjective, the 'objective achievement of salvation there and then and a subjective appropriation of it here and now'.[35] Having eliminated the distinction, Barth then had the option of casting salvation wholly in terms of the subjective or wholly in terms of the objective. With few modifications, he chose the latter. Significantly, sanctification is said to be synonymous with conversion[36] and this took place with and in our justification. 'The

God who in His humiliation justifies us is also the man who in His exaltation sanctifies us.'[37] It is, like justification, a 'transformation' or 'new determination' which has already taken place before the world; it has already happened *de jure*. Neither justification nor sanctification has been recognized *de facto* by all men but this in no way invalidates the fact that sanctification 'is effective and authoritative for all ... and not merely for the people of God, the saints'.[38] What therefore remains for a Christian is simply to acknowledge what has happened and to praise God.

Barth is troubled by the biblical expressions 'old nature' and 'new nature', since he finds no place for these in his understanding of sanctification. It is a small consolation to him that these expressions occur relatively infrequently. He replaces them with the image of male and female, but this is quite unsatisfactory. The essence of the male/female images in Scripture is that while there are differences of sex and role these occur within an essential complementarity. Male and female by design are compatible with one another and their differences are a mutual enhancement. The point of the old man/new man imagery is quite the reverse. It stresses differences, not compatibility, differences of time and quality. But once Barth has decided to interpret sanctification in an exclusively objective framework, biblical language is simply made to conform to his decision.

The atonement, then, has universal significance and faith neither adds to it nor takes away from it. All men are in Christ and all men are converted *de jure* before they exercise faith. Man is in God's fellowship regardless of his merits, demerits, desires, volitions or opinions. This is what the covenant of God intended and this is what Jesus achieved.

The definition of sin assumed by this treatment is rather unusual. Sin, Barth says, is a theological word. Its meaning is known only in relation to God. It is therefore only known through Christ. If sin is the absence of knowledge, then knowing Christ necessarily precedes it. 'If the law were given where the gospel is not yet given,' explains Wingren, 'it would imply that man as he encounters the gospel already through "the law" has a partial knowledge of God and His will, and thus the Word loses its position as Lord over Man.'[39] It therefore follows that the gospel precedes the law, a position which has proved particularly offensive to Lutherans who are the guardians of the distinction between and right relation of law and gospel.[40]

Barth's inversion of law and gospel means that a knowledge of sin is not the precondition of being converted. It also means that it is impossible, but for logical inconsistency, to make ethical pronouncements affecting those who have not yet acknowledged their justification and sanctification in Christ. This undercuts any Christian witness in society. It makes Barth's anaemic response to Marxism entirely comprehensible and his earlier, sterling opposition to Nazism somewhat enigmatic.[41]

Neither Barth nor Brunner will allow that man's hope of transcending death can legitimately be based on his worth.[42] If man is immortal it is because God has made him so, yet they part company in explaining how this is so. Brunner argues that what is immortal is the *imago Dei* which is the relation of man's inner being to God; it is this which transcends biological death.[43] The dissolution of the body, either in the case of man or of Christ, is relatively unimportant. If he acknowledges a final resurrection of the body, it is not in any way necessary to the completion of the relation with God, but rather it is merely a finishing touch to creation. On the other hand Barth, who does not believe that Jesus' body rotted in the grave and who sees mankind rising with him, has a different solution. It leads naturally into one of the more obscure corners of Barth's thought, that of universalism.

A variety of answers has been given to this issue within neo-orthodoxy. Brunner occasionally makes assertions that can be read in a universalistic vein, especially in his book *Eternal Hope,* but by and large he seems to lean towards the obliteration of those standing outside of a relationship to Christ. Aulén feels rather baffled by the problem and says that while there is the possibility that there will be some who are lost, faith 'cannot establish any definite propositions in this matter'.[44] And Barth irrationally affirms in some places that all have been predestined to be saved and, therefore, will be saved, and yet, in others, that some might be lost.

The elements that make up Barth's view are at least clear. It is mankind rather than certain individuals who are elect in Christ and the verdict of the resurrection is that his reprobation, which is also theirs, is complete. The covenant, and there is only one covenant, is thereby fulfilled through him. This is a covenant of grace and there is only one kind of grace, that which is redemptive. What Jesus did neither needs faith to complete it, nor is it invalidated by the absence of faith, since it has been finished decisively and objectively in his history. Paradoxically, however, Barth rejects a universal reconciliation of all things, and even if he has an objective universal atonement he seems to allow for the possibility that some might be able to slip beyond its efficacy. At the same time he can also affirm that the stream of grace is too strong and every dam of human resistance will be burst. Although Barth emits uncertain sounds on this matter it would certainly be correct to say that for him, all men are already in Christ even if Christ is not in all men, that not all have yet realized it, that it can confidently be hoped that all will, but there might be a possibility that some will not.[45]

Evaluation

The contribution of neo-orthodoxy in contemporary debate has had both its good and bad aspects. On the positive side, it must be said that these theologians have forced the Christian world to consider biblical themes that it once seemed had been set aside more or less permanently, such as the sovereign transcendence of God, the sin of man, his threatened destruction in the face of divine wrath, the divinity of Christ and his centrality in Christian thought. These are all themes whose appearance in Christian thought has varied in the past more or less in proportion to the seriousness with which Scripture has been taken. Neo-orthodoxy has largely rescued theology from the patronizing mentality of liberalism, but it has not altogether thrown off the influence of its parent, deep as its rebellion has been. Van Til, in his unusual way, made this point long ago of Barth.

If the new stress on the sovereign *agapē*-God is far more serious and worthy of reflection than what the liberals proposed in their visions of the kingdom, it is not, as Wingren has countered, altogether a satisfactory formulation. Authentic insights are present but the separation of love and law, the elimination of the penal motif, is an impoverishing development. Apparently Nygren has also sensed this, for Part II of his *Agape and Eros*, written some years after Part I, has made some corrections in the earlier conception. It is these corrections that make his understanding of the present aspect of salvation rather more satisfactory than in Aulén. But it remains to be said that Brunner's solid contribution in *The Mediator* is a necessary counterweight to the *agapē* theme which could itself easily become trivialized in the absence of a tight integration with law. This is seen best in the persistent tendency to underplay the reality of human guilt. If the words *guilt* or *condemnation* are employed it is often only in the sense of danger in the face of man's cosmic enemies. But man is not merely threatened by these oppressors; he also stands personally guilty before God in whom wrath is aroused.

The *Christus Victor* theme has, of course, been hailed as a great innovation, a seminal contribution to modern theology. What is not quite so clear is whether it is equally seminal in aiding us to elucidate the New Testament. Aulén's working methodology itself should and, indeed, has aroused suspicions on this score. His argument is that if the classic idea were present in the patristic period it is highly probable that it was also present in the New Testament.[46] Consequently Aulén works backwards from the early period into the New Testament looking there for the conclusions he has found elsewhere. Patristic scholars of no mean competence such as J. N. D. Kelly and H. E. W. Turner, however, have found only slender evidence for Aulén's conclusions in the patristic period, and telling evidence against them.[47] Likewise, there is a consensus among some scholars that the break in doctrinal continuity betweeen Luther and later Lutherans upon which Aulén insists has more to do with style than substance. And Luther himself increasingly is being seen as having penal elements in his thought.[48] Furthermore, Aulén's understanding of the Latin theory, not to mention the treatment of Anselm in particular, are too historically insensitive to pass muster. It might be more charitable to Aulén, then, to allow his theological thesis to stand by itself and merely to pass over the historical justification he has attempted to provide for it. Yet even this is not altogether satisfactory. Sin, after all, is much more than a power to be conquered. It is a blameworthy condition to be rectified because it incurs guilt in man and arouses wrath in God. Aulén's blindness to this side of the New Testament teaching has serious consequences for many other aspects of his thought. Not least, one notices an inevitable inclination toward universalism among all of those who held an unmodified and unbalanced classic view of the atonement.

Neither Aulén nor Barth is satisfactory on justification, although for different reasons. Aulén is obliged to use penal language but this is promptly modified, whereas Barth, who also uses it, invests it with new significance. Barth's refusal to identify the revelatory Word with the text of Scripture means that for him the three constitutive elements of justification are an unknown God, unknowing man and the Word which joins them. It should be countered, however, that this trilogy should be replaced by the works of God (natural revelation and an *imago Dei* which if tarnished is not destroyed) the works of man (sin and guilt) and the preached message of Christ's atonement as the point of connection. Yet plainly the notion of repentance as a condition of accepting the gospel, which is natural and necessary when sin's guilt is exposed by the law, is alien to Barth. The law for him follows rather than precedes the gospel and he is dubious about any elements of subjective appropriation. Undoubtedly he is right in seeing that there is an objective side to atonement which Paul calls reconciliation, propitiation and redemption. The means by which this is appropriated, however, is faith and the result is then justification. Faith, John Murray declares, 'is not directed to the fact that we have been justified but is directed to Christ in order that we may be justified'.[49]

Because of this confusion between the objective and subjective aspects of faith, there is an undisguised universalism present in much neo-orthodox writing. The grounds of this universalism, however, are new.

J. I. Packer has pointed out[50] that universal salvation is frequently based today, not on the benevolence of God or the inconsequence of sin, but on the triumph of Christ's cross. It is a universalism not of divine indifference but of divine conquest. Thus it is argued that God intends all to be saved, that he has made provision for all to be saved and if all are saved this will be so only because of Christ's work. Universalism and Christian particularism are thus not as incompatible as they have sometimes appeared, or so it is argued.

In general, biblical support for this view is claimed from those texts which point to God's universal design in salvation (1 Tim. 4:2; 2 Pet. 3:9), Christ's universal provision in the cross (2 Cor. 5:19; Col. 1:20; Tit. 2:11; Heb. 2:9; 1 Jn. 2:2) and the Bible's prediction of Christ's universal conquest (Acts 3:21; Jn. 12:32; Rom. 5:18, 19; 1 Cor. 15:22–28; Phil. 2:9–11; Eph. 1:10). Packer has countered, however, that all of these verses are susceptible of a different interpretation, that in many cases the immediate context includes phrases explicitly pointing away from this conclusion and that Scripture consistently conditions the offer of salvation to all men, making it effective to those who believe it, receive it, and obey it.

The most decisive evidence against this line of thought, however, is Jesus' own attitude. It is directly from him that the teaching arises that life's throngs will be divided into sheep and goats; the sheep will enter '*zoēn aiōnion*', and the goats, '*kolasin aiōnion*' (Mt. 25:46). The divided destinies correspond to the broad and narrow ways that lead to destruction and life respectively (Mt. 7:13–4). There are two types of people, those who build on sandy foundations and those who build on solid rock (Mt. 7:24–27). There is always a Rich Man and a Lazarus (Luke 16:19–31) in every community; there will always be a mansion (Jn. 14:2) and a Gehenna (Mt. 5:22; Mk. 9:42–48).

Jesus and the apostles who elaborated his teaching were either in ignorance of the Father's universal saving intent and its actual accomplishment through the cross, or they chose to dissemble this truth. If universalism is right, Jesus was either ill-informed or a liar. Neither option is very appealing.

The disturbed balance between the objective and subjective also persists throughout the discussions by these theologians on sanctification; what they have to say on the subject also tends to be rather sparse. Barth, of course, has a respectable section devoted to this theme, but it is soon discovered that the present aspect of it is virtually all subsumed under the past, conditional sanctification under positional.

Neo-orthodoxy has neither sustained the interest which it generated earlier, nor has it been able to control the direction of modern theology subsequent to World War II. This is probably due in part to some of the contradictory elements which it sought to synthesize, which led to uncertainty among its adherents and instability within the movement. In time, a clear choice seemed to force itself upon them. Either they would have to move in a more conservative direction as Barth himself vainly tried to do, or to proceed in a more existential direction as Bultmann had done.

The failure of neo-orthodoxy to relate to this world is also responsible for the dissolution of the movement. Oscar Cullman singled out

Barth's disappointing silence in the face of Marxism as particularly damaging. Nygren and Aulén defended this lack of coherent relation by insisting that this is still a time for antithesis, *diastasis*. This *lacuna* is partly addressed in the surprising Gifford Lectures Brunner gave,[51] but far more than this was needed to redress the imbalance successfully. The cavalier dismissal, in many instances, of salvation in its experiential dimension was really part of the same problem. When the attempted rectification came through Bultmann and Tillich it not only proved distasteful to Barth but took theology even farther from the conservative heritage from which it had partly arisen.

Notes

[1] The term neo-orthodox is vague and elastic. Consequently, other authors have referred to Tillich, Bultmann and the Niebuhrs as being 'neo-orthodox', whereas here the term is reserved for Barth, Brunner, Nygren and Aulén; in other words it is reserved for the movement's more conservative axis. In general, the term stands for those tendencies in theology which assert divine transcendence, see man's knowledge of God as given only by God himself, define revelation in terms of personal encounter rather than in propositions, see the Bible simply as an instrument of the Spirit, stress man's sinfulness and the judgment under which he labours and look to Christ to provide both salvation and revelation. In this sense it is generally more true to speak of Barth as neo-orthodox and Bultmann as existential, although they also have common elements.

[2] Nygren's assumption in this analysis is that 'motif research', rather than narrow lexicographical studies, is the surest way of finding a word's meaning. The researcher needs to set a word in its own broad context, within its own religious system, rather than making connections with other religious usages or engaging in minute linguistic studies. See Anders Nygren, *Agape and Eros* (Philadelphia, 1953), pp. 34–40. *Cf.* his *Meaning and Method: Prolegomena to a Scientific Philosophy of Religion and a Scientific Theology* (London and Philadelphia, 1972), pp. 371–376. *Cf.* Gustav Wingren, *Theology in Conflict* (Edinburgh and Philadelphia, 1958), pp. 85–107. See also his 'Swedish Theology since 1900', *Scottish Journal of Theology*, IX (June 1956), pp. 113–134.

[3] Theology is either theocentric or egocentric, according to Nygren, with no possible compromise or *via media* between these tendencies. An attempt to negotiate between this Scylla and Charybdis is Helmut Thielicke's *The Evangelical Faith* (Grand Rapids, 1974) where he distinguishes these tendencies as 'Cartesian' and 'non-Cartesian'.

[4] Anders Nygren, *Essence of Christianity* (Philadelphia, 1961), pp. 90–91.

[5] The close relationship between the nature of this atonement and the doctrine of God it presupposes is explored in Aulén's *The Drama and the Symbols: A Book on Images of God and the Problems they Raise* (London and Philadelphia, 1970).

[6] Gustav Aulén, *The Faith of the Christian Church* (Philadelphia, 1960: London, 1961), p. 182.

[7] Nels Ferré, *Swedish Contributions to Modern Theology* (New York, 1966), p. 144.

[8] Wingren, p. 119. If Wingren is correct that there are pervasive elements of Platonism in

Barth's thought, then there exists here a difference with the Lundensians, Nygren and Aulén, who have sharply opposed all forms of idealism.

[9] Karl Barth, *Church Dogmatics,* ed. G. W. Bromiley and T. F. Torrance (5 vols,; Edinburgh, 1936–69), IV, 1, p. 39. Henceforth Barth's work will be abbreviated as *CD.*

[10] The essence of the initial debate in 1934 appeared in two brief essays, Brunner's being entitled *Nature and Grace* and Barth's, *No!* Subsequently each has elaborated upon the positions taken there, Brunner in his *The Divine-Human Encounter, Revelation and Reason* and his *Dogmatics,* Barth in *CD.* Neither Nygren nor Aulén followed Barth in this matter.

[11] The use of the word 'fall' in this context is somewhat specialized, since neither Barth nor Brunner sees the first three chapters of Genesis as being historical; there was not an original couple, Adam and Eve, who were addressed by God and disobeyed his commandment.

[12] Barth, *CD,* IV, 1, pp. 22–66.

[13] Barth, *CD,* II, 2.

[14] 'In Him the fact is once for all established that God does not exist without man,' Barth has said. The consequence is that in Christ 'genuine deity includes in itself genuine humanity'. Karl Barth, *The Humanity of God* (Richmond, 1960: London, 1967), p. 47. *Cf.* Barth, *CD,* III, 2, pp. 55–324.

[15] Barth, *CD,* IV, 1, pp. 54–66.

[16] John Baillie, *Our Knowledge of God* (London, 1952), p. 25. *Cf.* J. D. Bettis, 'Theology in the Baillie Debate; Barth's Rejection of Natural Theology and the Hermeneutical Problem', *Scottish Journal of Theology,* 22 (December 1969), pp. 385–405.

[17] See G. C. Berkouwer, *The Triumph of Grace in the Theology of Karl Barth* (Grand Rapids and London, 1956), pp. 123–132.

[18] The cross is, of course, central to the thought of revelation for Aulén. It is an objective event but revelation is not static. It is fixed in Christ but continuing in the sense that the struggle against evil continues. Revelation is 'God's dramatic struggle to make himself known against an opposition of forces of evil' (Ferré, p. 101). See Aulén's essay on revelation in John Baillie and Hugh Martin, eds., *Revelation* (London and New York, 1937), pp. 275–310.

[19] 'Its central theme is the idea of the Atonement as a Divine conflict and victory ... God is pictured as in Christ carrying through a victorious conflict against powers of evil which are hostile to his will. This constitutes Atonement, because the drama is a cosmic drama, and the victory over the hostile powers brings to pass a new relation, a relation of reconciliation, between God and the world.' Aulén, *Christus Victor,* pp. 4, 5.

[20] Ferré, p. 133.

[21] Echoes of Aulén are found in Nygren, *Essence of Christianity,* pp. 117ff.; Anders Nygren, *Commentary on Romans* (London and Philadelphia, 1949), pp. 144–167.

[22] Barth, *CD,* IV, 1, pp. 122–357, 514–642.

[23] Donald Bloesch, *Jesus is Victor! Karl Barth's Doctrine of Salvation* (Nashville, 1976). The delineation of the classic motif in Barth and its consequences have been explored throughout the book, but especially the chapter 'Reinterpreting the Atonement'. See also Robert L. Raymond, *Barth's Soteriology* (Philadelphia, 1967); J. L. Scott, 'Covenant in the Theology of Karl Barth', *Scottish Journal of Theology,* 17 (June 1964), pp. 182–198. A comparable position is maintained by Donald Baillie who likewise affirms the classic motif but allows modified penal elements a small role. The rejection of a full penal understanding is based largely on C. H. Dodd's discussions of propitiation. See Baillie's *God was in Christ: An Essay in Incarnation and Atonement* (London and New York, 1948), pp. 197–202, 187–189.

[24] The objective emphasis in Barth has led him to insist that the supernatural dimension in Christ's cross occurs within the tissue of his own empirical history. Thus while Barth distinguishes two types of history – *Historie* and *Geschichte* – he argues, to Bultmann's bafflement, that they cannot be separated. In this he received substantial support in the exegetical work of Oscar

Cullmann, especially in his *Salvation in History* (New York, 1965: London, 1970), pp. 186–291. See also Oscar Cullmann, 'Out of Season Remarks on the "Historical Jesus" of the Bultmann School', *Union Seminary Quarterly Review*, 16 (January 1961), pp. 131–148.

[25] Emil Brunner, *Dogmatics* (3 vols., London, 1949: Philadelphia, 1950), II, p. 285.

[26] Brunner, *The Mediator*, p. 25.

[27] *Ibid.*, p. 467.

[28] *Ibid.*, p. 578.

[29] Brunner's existential concerns are closer to Bultmann at this point than to Barth, for the latter professedly abandoned this element after his first, ill-fated attempt to write his theology. Brunner's distinctive emerges in particular in *The Divine-Human Encounter*. The adopted epistemological structure is the Buberian 'I-Thou' in which God as Subject meets man as subject in 'personal' relation, rather than standing over against man as Object.

[30] Aulén, *The Faith of the Church*, p. 144.

[31] *Ibid.*, p. 265.

[32] *Ibid.*, pp. 256–262.

[33] Gustav Aulén, *Reformation and Catholicity* (Philadelphia, 1961: Edinburgh, 1962), p. 63.

[34] Barth, *CD*, IV, 2, p. 502.

[35] *Ibid.*, pp. 502, 503.

[36] Two different German words are translated as 'conversion'. *Umkehr* corresponds to what is in view in the term 'positional sanctification'; *Bekehren* corresponds to 'conditional sanctification', that is, the experiential aspect of exercising faith. The latter is given an insignificant place in Barth's thought. His chief concern is with the world's dying in Christ, the separation of humanity from its own sin and hence its objective reversal and turning to God through Christ. That this has happened *de jure* is of far greater import to Barth than that men have realized it *de facto*.

[37] Barth, *CD*, IV, 2 p. 503.

[38] *Ibid.*, p. 518.

[39] Wingren, p. 34.

[40] See, for example, Robert D. Preus, 'Doctrine of Justification and Reconciliation in the Theology of Karl Barth', *Concordia Theological Monthly*, 31 (April 1960), pp. 236–244; T. Coates, 'Barthian Inversion; Gospel and Law', *Concordia Theological Monthly*, 26, No. 7 (July 1955), pp. 481–491; Jacques Rossel, 'From a Theology of Crisis to a Theology of Revolution? Karl Barth, Mission and Missions', *Ecumenical Review*, XXI, No. 3 (July 1969), pp. 204–215.

[41] Barth's ethics and the role they might play in society have been assessed rather differently. Some have seen him as a budding Marxist and potential revolutionary who laid the groundwork for the new 'political theology', whereas others have tended to focus on the muted and quiescent aspects in this thought. For brief summaries see G. A. Butler, 'Karl Barth and Political Theology', *Scottish Journal of Theology*, 22 (November 1974), pp. 441–458; R. W. Palmer, 'Methodological Weaknesses in Barth's Approach to Ethics', *Journal of Religious Thought*, 62, No. 1 (1969), pp. 70–82. Niebuhr has probably assessed the impact of Barth's position correctly when he says that in the interest of stressing 'the ultimate religious fact of the sinfulness of man', he undermines the day-to-day moral judgments that have to be made and has great difficulty 'in achieving a measure of political sanity and justice'. Reinhold Niebuhr, *The Nature and Destiny of Man* (2 vols.; London, 1941, 1943: New York, 1949), I, p. 220.

[42] G. M. Schurr, 'Brunner and Barth on Life after Death', *Journal of Religious Thought*, 24 (1967–68), pp. 95–110.

[43] For Brunner, the soul disintegrates with the body; what survives, the *imago Dei*, survives only as it stands in relation to God, the eternal Subject.

[44] Aulén, *The Faith of the Church*, p. 154.

[45] Bromiley has sought to soften this aspect of Barth's thought by pointing out that he is not

an express universalist and that the tendencies in this direction stem from the laudable desire to make reconciliation objective. See his essay entitled 'Karl Barth' in Philip Edgcumbe Hughes, ed., *Creative Minds in Contemporary Theology* (Grand Rapids, 1966), pp. 54, 55. Having compared Barth's views with biblical teaching, however, Colin Brown concluded that the universalism in his thought provided a 'procrustean bed' on which the Bible was laid and what did not fit was simply lopped off. See his *Karl Barth and the Christian Message* (London, 1967), pp. 135–139.

[46] 'We should have a right to expect a priori that the view of the Fathers would be also that of the New Testament.' Aulén, *Christus Victor*, p. xiv.

[47] J. N. D. Kelly in his *Early Christian Doctrines* (New York, 1959: London, fourth edition, 1968), pp. 163–188, simply describes the patristic outlook, but finds ideas which Aulén overlooked; H. E. W. Turner, however, addresses Aulén's thesis directly, arguing that if the motif is present it is there in a far more complex fashion than Aulén has realized. See his *The Patristic Doctrine of Redemption: A Study of the Development during the First Five Centuries* (London, 1952), pp. 48–61.

[48] E.g. see Ian D. Kingston Siggins, *Martin Luther's Doctrine of Christ* (New Haven, 1970) pp. 108–143; E. R. Fairweather, 'Incarnation and Atonement; an Anselmian Response to Aulén's *Christus Victor*', *Canadian Journal of Theology*, VII, No. 3 (July 1961), pp. 167–175.

[49] Murray's reasoning is as follows: 'According to Paul we are justified by faith, and to apply the terms for justification without discrimination to anything else than to that which is correlative with faith and therefore coincident with it is to deviate radically from the sustained emphasis of the apostle. It is true that there is the once-for-all accomplishment in the blood of Christ which is antecedent to faith. Paul calls it the propitiation, the reconciliation, and redemption. But the all-but uniform, if not uniform, use of the term 'justification' and its equivalent is to designate that judgment of God of which faith is the instrument.... It is not to be assumed that in the epistle to the Romans the terms *dikaiosynē, dikaiōsis, dikaiōma* are used synonymously, as Barth apparently assumes (*cf.* p. 20). In 5:16 *dikaiōma* and in 5:18 *dikaiōsis* refer to God's justifying act. But exegesis neither requires nor allows identification of this act with the *dikaiosynē Theou* of 1:17; 3:21, 22; 10:3. The latter is the justifying righteousness but is to be distinguished from the justifying act.' (Greek transliterations mine.) John Murray, *The Epistle to the Romans: The English Text with Introduction, Exposition, and Notes* (2 vols., London and Grand Rapids, 1968–71), I, p. 385; See also his review of Barth's *Christ and Adam* in *Westminster Theological Journal*, 20 (May 1958), pp. 198–203.

[50] James I. Packer, 'The Way of Salvation, Part III: The Problems of Universalism', *Bibliotheca Sacra*, 130 (January 1973), pp. 3–11.

[51] Emil Brunner, *Christianity and Civilization* (2 vols., London, 1948–49). See also his essay 'Critic or Apologist of Civilization?' *Religion in Life*, XXX, No. 3 (Summer, 1951), pp. 323–328.

Bultmann believes in Jesus Christ, not *the only Son of God, (yet) our Lord; who was* not *conceived by the Holy Ghost,* not *born of the Virgin Mary, suffered under Pontius Pilate; was crucified, dead and buried; he did* not *descend into hell; the third day he is (thought to have) risen again from the dead; he did* not *ascend into heaven; sitteth* not *at the right hand of God the Father Almighty; from thence he shall* not *come to judge the quick and the dead.*

Cited by R. A. Egon Hessel

If one is to be true to the modern view of the world, one cannot build more history into the system than Bultmann does.

Norman Perrin

One wonders where the left-wing existential theologians have found their 'modern man'.

Paul van Buren

Professor: 'Dr Tillich, are you not a dangerous man?' Dr Tillich: 'Yes.'

Chapter Three

The existential approach

Classical liberalism was initially rebutted by a unified neo-orthodoxy. Neo-orthodoxy, however, soon bifurcated into two quite separate schools. The point at issue was how well Christian faith accorded with existential philosophy and to what extent it might be reinterpreted in these terms. Barth and Bultmann reached different conclusions and those associated with them made it clear where those differences lay. Not only so, but the principals themselves reacted against one another and in the process moved off some of the common ground they had both formerly occupied. Barth began to disavow Kierkegaard; Bultmann began to embrace Heidegger. Bultmann's theological interest became increasingly subjective; Barth's became increasingly objective. Barth distinguished between *Geschichte* ('super' history, the realm where God works which is grasped not by research but by faith) and *Historie* (ordinary history, the web of events linked by natural cause and effect in human life which is comprehended by reason),[1] but insisted that the former occurred *within* the latter; Bultmann also distinguished between these two types of history but insisted that the former could occur *without* the latter. Thus, Barth believed in Jesus' bodily resurrection but refused to tie any theological affirmation to its facticity on the grounds that it is *Geschichte* and not *Historie* which is important; Bultmann believed in 'resurrection' but denied that this involved Jesus' bodily resurrection *(Historie)* and accepted merely its existential meaning *(Geschichte)* for the contemporary person. Those who had been joined together against a common opponent thus divided against themselves.[2]

The attempt to interpret Christianity existentially has been undertaken by a distinguished group of theologians, only two of whom will receive attention in this chapter, namely Rudolf Bultmann and Paul Tillich. To these names we could also add those of Friedrich Gogarten, a Lutheran scholar who participated with Barth in the original overthrow of liberalism, and Fritz Buri who has, perhaps, given the most radical interpretation to Bultmann's programme of demythologization. In the nature of the case, existential theologies tend to be highly individualistic and therefore it is difficult, if not perilous, to attempt to group them together and provide a single summary of their conclusions. On the other hand, Bultmann and Tillich, despite the idiosyncratic form of their writings, do serve well as representatives of this approach. In America, H. Richard and Reinhold Niebuhr have also been prominent existential theologians, but their efforts have been expended less on theology as such and more on political, sociological and ethical matters.

In Bultmann's thought there is an interplay of substance from three often separate disciplines, a situation which is not duplicated in Tillich's case. For if Bultmann's instincts are primarily historical, his findings with respect to the New Testament data are heavily influenced by the Heideggerian philosophy which he has assimilated.[3] It is his philosophy which has led him, it would seem, to his sceptical conclusions about the historical Jesus and it is these conclusions which lie behind his hermeneutical proposal – offered from the viewpoint of a New Testament scholar – that Scripture should be demythologized. The range of Tillich's interests is broader in terms of subject matter but the means by which he reaches his conclusions is simpler. He is a philosopher who is working with Christian materials, but he does have a passing interest in biblical criticism, the results of which he accepts as a matter of course. His historical abilities are not, by comparison with Bultmann, quite as developed nor his judgments as reliable.[4]

Bultmann and Tillich do, however, share an approach to theology which springs from existential assumptions; more precisely, it springs from Heidegger's existential assumptions although Tillich has developed these into the area of ontology far more fully than has Bultmann.

Existentialism, to put it very simply, is concerned with delineating authentic from inauthentic existence. Authentic existence is what results when a person's full potential is realized; to the degree to which this does not happen, this person is living an inauthentic existence. The full potential in most people is not realized because they willingly allow themselves to be caught in the web of an objective world where they enjoy the safety of being more or less an object, seldom ever having to affirm themselves by decision or expose themselves to risk. They make the world around them predictable and their future safe. The mystery of their own being they extinguish precisely because it is neither subject to their reason nor can it be contained within their understanding. They are more like spectators at a play than active participants in it or, to change the image, they are like Kierkegaard's drunken peasant who journeys home on his cart oblivious to his own existence.

There are, then, two types of knowledge that we have about ourselves, the one objective and the other subjective.[5] The first relates to the body and is gained by measurement, inspection, and analysis. It is the way of science. Its tools are observation and applied reason; the condition of success is that kind of accuracy that comes from care and an appropriate detachment from the subject under analysis. The second arises, not from the material aspect of man, but from his spiritual consciousness, his loves, hopes, fears, needs, perceptions and desires. None of these can be probed, measured, weighed or otherwise scientifically inspected. Here reason is futile and detachment injurious, even if it were possible.

Existentialism in all of its forms – atheistic, theistic and Christian – therefore affirms, first, that reality cannot be grasped by reason and, second, that the subjective consciousness is the proper focus of philosophical activity. Yet it should be said that it is less a philosophy with fixed conclusions than a way of philosophizing, less an arguable 'truth' than a way of existing. That is why thinkers as diverse as Nietzsche and Dostoevsky, Blake and Kierkegaard, Socrates and Jaspers have all been spoken of as being existential.

The historical Jesus

Both Tillich and Bultmann begin by disengaging Christian faith from the historical Jesus.[6] The route which each takes is rather different, but the reason is the same. If faith is tied into the known, objective world the outcome can only be that kind of inauthentic existence from which people need to be delivered.

Bultmann is, in fact, doubtful – but the grounds he gives for his doubt are historical rather than philosophical – whether much can be salvaged regarding the actual life, personality and teaching of Jesus. Jesus himself wrote nothing and his biographers who were indifferent to these matters have, instead, given us imaginative reconstructions of the events, couched in terms of a primitive view of life no longer credible in the twentieth century. These accounts tell us more about their authors' 'faith' than the affairs they seem to be recording. What can be ascertained is that Jesus did live, did enter Jerusalem and was executed. He apparently regarded himself as a Jewish prophet whose central message was the imminent demise of the world. It was his followers rather than Jesus himself who introduced the idea that he was Isaiah's Suffering Servant and that he would return to the world again. Jesus ascribed the *parousia,* not to himself, but to the mythical Son of man.

If Jesus is unimportant for Christian faith, Bultmann nevertheless affirms that he is indispensable to a full understanding of New Testament theology. Jesus' message, is '*a* presupposition for the theology of the New Testament rather than a part of that theology itself' (my italics), the others being, as Jeremias has pointed out, 'the Easter experience of the disciples, the Jewish Messianic expectations, the mythology of the pagan world which provided the garment with which Jesus of Nazareth was to be clothed'.[7]

Similarly, Tillich argues that our knowledge of Jesus, the *historisch* figure, is limited because the New Testament picture we have of him is given by 'persons who had received him as the Christ' and who consequently blurred what they saw. The work of the Bultmann school, Tillich says, succeeded in awakening the Barthians from their historical slumbers, but he is doubtful that there has emerged any 'picture behind the biblical one which could be made scientifically probable'.[8] The historical figure, a somewhat undistinguished Galilean peasant, is now lost in obscurity.

The disappearance of Jesus, however, by no means marks the demise of Christian faith, for this faith, apart from accepting the bare existence of Jesus, is in no other way tied to him. 'Christianity was born,' Tillich affirms, 'not with the birth of the man who is called "Jesus", but in a moment in which one of his followers was driven to say to him, "Thou are the Christ".'[9] The faith operative in his early followers expressed itself in their mythological conceptions such as

Son of David, Son of man, heavenly man, Messiah, Son of God, Kyrios, Logos.

'Son of man' Jesus used of himself, Tillich says, not to convey the idea that a heavenly being left that existence to become 'transmuted into a man' which would result only in a 'half-god' and is anyway an 'absurd story', but rather as designating 'an original unity between God and man'.[10] 'Son of God' similarly discloses this essential unity in the New Being. The title, however, is not applied exclusively to Jesus. He was merely the first to overcome the conditions of estranged existence in himself — Tillich's definition of sin — and thus as he grew into divinity exhibited in himself the New Being. Others, however, can follow in his steps. Throughout his discussion of these terms, Tillich strives to show how the literal belief in a transcendent God who clothed himself in human flesh came about and how untenable it is. All of these terms are symbolic statements which cannot be grasped literally but must be appropriately interpreted. The result quite clearly is to float Christian faith free of the historical Jesus, about whom there can be no certain knowledge, and to place the locus of belief in the existential 'Christ'.

The meaning of salvation

The second notion shared by both Bultmann and Tillich is that the New Testament teaching on salvation is mythological. The word *myth* is peculiarly Bultmann's but Tillich is in general agreement with the idea. Bultmann does not mean by it something which is blatantly erroneous and which should be dismissed out of hand. Rather, he has in mind the way in which the first Christians clothed and communicated the content of the invisible world by means of the visible.[11] It is the inner content — what he calls the kerygma — which is enduring, but its shell is not in its literal form. The task of New Testament exegesis is to strip away the shell, find the kernel and then reclothe it in terms comprehensible to people living in a technological age. For Bultmann this means accepting the fact that the universe is a closed system operating under the uniformity of cause and effect. This is an assumption he thinks is held by most twentieth-century people. The New Testament must be shorn of those aspects of belief which are not compatible with it. With respect to soteriology this means rejecting the ideas of heaven and hell, angels which are good and bad, the incarnation of the second person of the Godhead, his virgin birth, sinlessness, atoning death, resurrection, ascension, second coming, the traditional doctrine of the Trinity, the personality of the Holy Spirit, original sin and death as its consequence. Tillich is sympathetic to this emasculation, but he has realized, in a way that Bultmann apparently has not, that contemporary secularism is quite as much a myth' as the 'primitive' world-view which is being discarded. Religious language is such, Tillich argues, that man can never speak of God in any other way than that which is merely symbolic.[12] If Tillich is right, this does mean that on his assumptions at least, Bultmann's own views are in need of being demythologized quite as much as those of the New Testament.

It would be a serious blunder to think that Bultmann has arrived at such opinions out of ignorance as to what Scripture affirms. There are, Philip Hughes has rightly said, 'few religious thinkers of our day who have shown a deeper understanding and offered a more stimulating exegesis of the theology of the New Testament'[13] than has he. The important point for Bultmann, however, is not what it says, but what it *means;* more precisely, what it means for contemporary people. The question of hermeneutics in his thought overshadows simple exegesis.

What does the New Testament have to say about salvation? Unlike conservative theologians, Bultmann sees no unity between the Testaments and none within them. As a leading exponent of form criticism, he sees different traditions within the New Testament which give different answers to this question. These traditions are associated especially with the Palestinian Christians, Hellenistic circles, Paul and post-Pauline developments. And he is certain that within these circles Christian faith began, not with Jesus, but with his followers, not in his life but after his death. Jesus is significant, not as the founder of one of the world's great religions, but because in him, chosen arbitrarily by God as he was, something unique happened as a response to which the great religion arose after his death.[14] There is, then, a large measure of disjuncture between the Gospels and Epistles which profoundly affects the way in which salvation is conceived.

Among the various contributors to the New Testament corpus it is to Paul that we look as the 'founder of Christian theology'. It is he who has explored most effectively the assumptions of Hellenistic faith and with his imaginative use of gnostic myths and mysteries has provided us with a full-orbed soteriology.

According to Bultmann, Paul sees man as always driven by a desire for something lying beyond his experience in the pursuit of which he either loses or finds his self.[15] To find one's self is to cease to live off one's own resources; to lose one's self is to attempt to displace God from this world but in so doing one merely hands one's self over to death.[16] Man has done this consistently and persistently so that the world which was made for him and his good has become his destroyer.

The presupposition of the change from death to life is justification.[17] There can be no doubt, says Bultmann, that for Paul *dikaiosynē* was a forensic term that spoke of an acquittal or a favourable standing accorded a person in the eyes of the law, regardless of his actual guilt or innocence. In theology, then, this imputed righteousness is not an ethical quality a person possesses, nor an attained sinlessness, but a relationship to God which is of such a nature that the guilty person is viewed as innocent. For such a person, the old course of the world died with Christ and in him he has been delivered from it. Justification is therefore closely paralleled by the doctrines of adoption, reconciliation and redemption in its present aspect.

Reconciliation is one of the themes in Paul's soteriology. Bultmann does not see Paul doing what Barth does, namely, using it as an umbrella under which many other doctrines can be crowded. What he says by way of exegeting Paul confirms many of the conclusions reached by conservative theologians. Reconciliation presupposes that a prior alienation between two parties existed and has been overcome, that the breach has been healed. Nowhere is the divine initiative more evident than here, for the healing of the breach, which takes place factually and objectively in Paul's view, is accomplished without man's efforts and, indeed, even without his knowledge. He is simply presented with a *fait accompli* and invited to receive it. In this understanding of salvation, human *erōs* is denied and all the achievements have to be ascribed to divine *agapē*. It is this *agapē* which simply presents man with the consequence: 'Will you surrender, utterly surrender, to God's dealing – will you know yourself to be a sinner before God?'[18]

The work of Christ, Bultmann acknowledges, is explained by Paul in images that are penal or sacrificial. Yet he points out that Paul is not only interested in the thought of how guilt is cancelled by vicarious atonement, but places alongside this the motif of conquest. Christ's death, for Paul, is 'the means of release from the powers of this age: Law, Sin and Death'.[19] Jesus' death and resurrection therefore have both a personal and a cosmic significance. But to elicit this significance, Paul made use of gnostic ideas, 'because through them the salvation-occurrence could be interpreted as actually happening to and for and in man'.[20]

The Christian who has entered the body of Christ and participated in the benefits of his death through baptism is now, of course, living between two ages. The old aeon has been terminated, but the new has not been fully realized. Freedom from sin, law and death are, however, its outcome as the believer looks for the imminent return of Christ. This event will terminate the world's life and should be seen as 'the completion and confirmation of the eschatological occurrence which has now already begun'.[21]

Bultmann's elaboration of New Testament soteriology is both precise and erudite, but his conclusions only establish the parameters and content of its authors' faith and not of his own. Indeed, how could New Testament belief serve as a norm for his faith? These early believers were working with a primitive cosmology which incorporated legendary elements, superstitious ideas and simply erroneous notions. The twentieth-century person can in no way participate in these beliefs. The question, therefore, that needs to be settled is how New Testament teaching can be translated into the contemporary vernacular and address modern man within the cosmology which he has assumed.

What, then, is the enduring nut within this outward and dispensable shell? Heidegger, Bultmann believed, has sometimes enabled us to understand the New Testament authors better than they understood themselves. And certainly their view of man at least runs parallel to, if it does not actually converge upon, contemporary, existential ideas.

The New Testament view of man is not that he is a fixed conglomerate of separate parts — body, mind and spirit — a kind of static amalgam. Man is a whole, an integrated unit, which is also plastic, fluid, malleable, changing and being changed by the decisions he makes. It is in the midst of this flux that his existence emerges as either authentic or inauthentic, either as a realization of his true potential – pictured in the Bible as the *imago Dei* – or a departure from what he really is.

Consequently he is faced with a choice every day as to whether he will live off his own resources or off God's. It is a choice between faith and nihilism, between being fixed within the safe but depersonalizing structures of the world or taking the risk of opening himself to a future which is unpredictable.[22] To find safety in the world, however, is to rely on something other than God and hence to commit idolatry. Idolatry brings with it its own darkness and despair. By contrast, to refuse all objective props of sight or reason is to enter into the 'life' of which John spoke. God and the world, faith and self, are separate and separating paths.

It has, of course, been asked what Christian faith can do for a person in Bultmann's thought which Heidegger is unable to do. Does the 'authentic' existence to which Bultmann strives really differ from that outlined by Heidegger? The form, Bultmann contends, is the same, but the content differs, for a Christian must affirm that this existence is attained not by human reason or effort but by divine grace. Christian existentialism, agrees Macquarrie, differs from atheistic existentialism in that 'it is God who gives to man the *existentiell* possibility of authentic being. . . . The transition from fallen to authentic existence is the work of God, not man.'[23]

More precisely, then, what is this 'work of God' and how does it operate in human life? God began this 'work' in Jesus despite the fact that in Bultmann's theology, he is stripped of all supernatural elements. But this is exactly why Christianity is scandalous. God has not addressed mankind from within its own rising consciousness but rather through an obscure prophet whom he chose almost at random. And through this Jesus, 'everyone is addressed and asked if he is willing to hear God's message of forgiveness and grace here'.[24]

Everyone is addressed in particular as they hear the preached Word which extends the 'Christ-event' into the present. Bultmann's use of *Word,* however, is somewhat varied and his readers are left to decide from the context whether he means by this the truth of the biblical text, God breaking through in the activity of the sermon, or the existential truth which language, as a participant in Being, mystically bears. But it is clear that for him 'the salvation-occurrence' as he puts it, is present 'in the "word" '.[25] Jesus, through the act of preaching, becomes the Christ over and over again. The incarnation, as it were, becomes a present reality to which we are audible witnesses rather than being merely a past event which was witnessed historically.

The cross, likewise, is not to be thought of as an objective act of God accomplished at a certain point in time and space but as the encounter between the image of that event and the individual. The event itself was just an execution like any other execution. The encounter with the image of this event, however, is what has the power to liberate us from the world in which we participate by reason and introduces us to that in which we live by 'faith'. In short, there were no ontological exchanges between Father and Son at Golgotha. It therefore follows, says Cullmann, that in Bultmann's thought salvation does not 'reside in the unique act, in Christ's death on the cross, but is an event repeated ever anew in each individual, whenever the message of the death of Christ addresses itself to him'.[26]

The resurrection is also given an existential rather than an *historisch* meaning by Bultmann. He is, of course, rather dubious as to whether there are any elements of truth in the gospel accounts of Jesus' resurrection and sees these accounts merely as 'myth'. The 'resurrection' which is affirmed by the Christian is that perception of things by which the old aeon and self dies and the new aeon and man begins. Jesus, Barth has said of Bultmann, was not raised 'for us' but is, instead, raised 'in us'.[27]

Finally, the *parousia* receives similar treatment, for it is Bultmann's contention that since there is no precedent for either the resurrection or the *parousia* they cannot be seen as literal events. If they were literal events they would breach the existent pattern of natural cause and effect; they would be exceptions to it.[28] And since Bultmann argues that Jesus never made any prediction about his own return to the world but only about that of the Son of man (a prediction which was proved incorrect), it follows that eschatology should as a whole be reinterpreted personally, focusing not on the world's end but our own. Indeed, Paul has given us the tools to do this in his assertion that the new age, in which we are participants, has already begun. Eschatology, which stresses God's transcendence, explains how our decisions about him become ultimate. That kind of decision, Paul Minear has said, which is the 'occasion for losing life and finding it, for becoming what in God's grace he already is – a new man' is 'an eschatological occasion'.[29]

When Bultmann speaks of being 'open to the future,' however, it needs to be recalled that he is not speaking of any *certain* future. It is inauthentic existence which desires the certainty of a known future. The only matter about which man can be sure is his own death and the only thing about which he should be concerning himself is the existential present. To a dying man, then, one offers no hope but only the exhortation to believe in God.

Tillich also gives the whole range of soteriological concerns a similarly existential treatment. Like Bultmann, he sees salvation as the process of becoming whole, of being healed and, he could as easily have said, of realizing hidden and lost potential. The word *salvation*, he says, is derived from *salvus*, 'healed'. In this sense, 'healing means reuniting that which is estranged, giving a center to what is split, overcoming the split between God and man, man and his world, man and himself'.[30] This 'split', as Tillich inelegantly calls it, is not, however, what conservative theology has in mind when it speaks of 'sin', 'wrath' and 'condemnation'. For these, too, are symbols that need to be decoded for the contemporary person.

For 'sin', Tillich substitutes the word *estrangement*, by which he means man's separation from the ground of his being. It is an estrangement captured in the biblical symbols of man's ejection from paradise, the confusion of tongues at Babel or Paul's statement about men who perverted the image of God into an idol. There is no historical point at which this began; simply to exist is to be estranged and to experience 'personal guilt and universal tragedy'.[31] Although Tillich has given a more extreme statement to divine transcendence than most theologians, ironically he is close to Schleiermacher in his notion of the 'ground' of one's being. It is almost as if he sees God working by, with and under all human personality as in a sacrament. From this reality man is initially alienated but to it he can be united. The resultant unification he describes as the 'New Being.' It was of this that Jesus was the pioneer. Yet plainly the reunification is not dependent upon the veracity of anything which Jesus said or did. Consequently, Tillich was far more appreciative of the other great religions than Bultmann. Christianity differs from other systems not so much in kind as in degree as it seeks to articulate the meaning of the mystery at the heart of human life.[32]

How, more precisely, is a person saved? According to Tillich this occurs in three stages which he describes as participation in, acceptance of and transformation by the New Being. These stages correspond to regeneration, justification and sanctification. Regeneration, he argues, is the new 'state of things universally' which the individual 'enters'; it is quite erroneous for a preacher to 'create emotional reactions' by appealing to each person individually. Rather, there is a changed existence designated as 'Christ' which the individual enters. It is this entrance that overcomes the results of estrangement, so we experience 'faith instead of unbelief, surrender instead of *hubris,* love instead of concupiscence'.[33] Justification which follows regeneration is God's act of accepting man in the New Being despite his condition of estrangement. What the 'atonement' declares is not, of course, that the exchange for man of divine righteousness for human sin through the cross has occurred, but 'that man's salvation is not dependent on the state of his development'. Sanctification is that process by which the New Being transforms personality and overcomes sin. It takes place both inside and outside the church. Tillich's purview is broad enough to see 'both the religious and the secular realm' as being divinely transformed in this manner just as he does of regeneration.

With respect to the future he both shared Bultmann's views and yet went beyond them. Man's only certainty in the future is his own death. And while Tillich could preach sermons rich with affirmation about the resurrection of the dead, he was dealing only with the necessary symbols by which we must communicate with one another about things divine. There is, in fact, no life after death. This is his conclusion as it is the presupposition of his entire system. There is, as Ferré has stated it, 'no transcendent realm, only transcendent meaning'. How it is possible to have 'meaning' which is not rooted in and derived from a known 'transcendent realm' is an enigma which his system sought to address. It is not surprising, however, to note that several of the 'death of God' theologians saw him as their father; Thomas Altizer and William Hamilton appropriately dedicated their book, *The Death of God,* to him.

Evaluation

Existential theology has attempted to rectify a deficiency which it has perceived in Barthianism. Whereas Barthian neo-orthodoxy stresses that all men are in Christ, existential theology has explored what it means to say that Christ is in men. To do this it has utilized the tool of existentialism which Barth has repudiated, and it has accepted secular assumptions about the world which Barth partly challenged. Insofar as both types of theology are built on narrow insights into the meaning of salvation – the one its objective side, the other its subjective – each represents an unhealthy extreme, neither is therefore satisfactory, and both have proved unstable in the *milieu* of contemporary thought. They are each fading and failing expressions of theology's attempt to be true to itself while being relevant to the modern world. Given this tension it would be correct to say as a rough generalization that Barth's approach was to see the modern world from the vantage point of a truncated Christian faith, whereas Bultmann and Tillich have seen Christian faith from the perspective of a 'modern' who finds it impossible to believe in miracles. Barth fails to relate his Christian faith to the contemporary world, while Bultmann and Tillich fail to make contact with the original biblical faith.

Nowhere is this deficiency in existential theology more obvious than in its attitude to the *historisch* person, Jesus. It is ironical that Bultmann, who has written a book about Jesus, insists on severing Christian faith from him. It thus becomes clear that all of his research into the Gospel traditions is not so much, as Hermann Diem has noted, to find a lost historical base for Christian faith, but to make sure that one cannot be found. Bultmann himself declares that Jesus never meets us in the preached Word, the *kerygma*, but Christ does. Christ is not Jesus. It is this disjuncture which has led David Cairns to note that though Bultmann's sermons are infused with profound thoughts about Christian faith he has cut away every reason for others to think that they are true, for the bridge between Jesus and Christ has been demolished.

Bultmann has denied that it was his intention to sever the historical Jesus from Christian faith, but his immediate followers have sensed that this is the outcome of his position and some of them have expressed their fears about the consequences. Among these 'post-

Bultmannians' who have engaged in a new quest for the historical Jesus are Günther Bornkamm, Herbert Braun, Hans Conzelmann, Erich Dinkler, Gerhard Ebeling, Ernst Fuchs, Ernst Käsemann and James Robinson. Their efforts to retrieve some of the elements of christology with which Bultmann dispensed can be dated from Käsemann's address at Marburg in 1953 and the two and a half decades which have followed have been filled with literary activity. It is doubtful, however, whether enough territory has yet been recaptured.

They still assert as if it were a matter beyond debate that Jesus' biographers had no interest in his humanity. Ralph Martin has pointed out, however, that scholars such as T. W. Manson, Vincent Taylor and A. M. Hunter have shown the existence of a high degree of interest on their part in Jesus' earthly life and the content of his teaching. Furthermore, they have not only seen these as part and parcel of authentic Christianity, but have questioned whether 'the first generations of Gentile believers were content to commit their lives to a mythological Lord whose "history" was (on the form-critical claim) as uncertain and adventitious as that of the cult divinities of the Hellenistic mystery religions.'[34]

Tillich's theology addresses the question of what a Christian could say if it were ever proved that Jesus had never lived. His answer is not always clear, for sometimes he argues that there is a 'factual element' in the Gospel narrative, but at other times he can brusquely dismiss this idea, saying that whether Jesus ever lived or not is a matter of indifference to him. Certainly he sets apart the 'truth of faith' from 'the truth of history,' the former being certain and sure, the latter being at best only probable and at worst defective.

The issue posed by the existentialists, therefore, can be boiled down to a simple question: 'Does Christ save me because he is the Son of God or is he the Son of God because he saves me?' Bultmann and Tillich both opt for the second alternative. Christology, therefore, has nothing to do with the historical Jesus, but it has to do with preaching, and, as Paul Althaus puts it, 'is therefore a reflexion about oneself, a thinking through of one's own existence'.[35] This is an impoverishing conception. In denying that the historical figure of Jesus can be meaningful to the modern world, existential theology shelters its private perceptions from any objective controls. Is it ever possible to know whether these subjective reflections are authentic or inauthentic? Is it or is it not 'God' who has broken through the sermon? To be sure, Bultmann's and Tillich's dismissal of personalized evil in the world does make these questions easier to answer, but the simplicity of their replies is an indication of the danger of their solution.

The refusal to allow the person and teachings of Jesus to establish the centre and norm of soteriology and the arbitrary manner in which the Gospel narrative is demythologized have seriously affected what is unique to Christian faith. After a dispassionate analysis of Tillich's theology and especially his ontology, Paul Edwards, who describes himself as an unbeliever, declares that it is 'compatible with anything whatever',[36] a point inadvertently conceded by Tillich himself in his attitude to non-Christian religions.

For both Tillich and Bultmann, Christianity is little more than an atemporal, unhistorical, subjective insight which repeats itself over and over in the lives of its adherents. This, of course, is remarkably like the gnosticism against which apostolic Christianity rebelled. It is Bultmann, rather than Paul, who is the gnostic.[37]

The refusal to incorporate the historic Jesus, his words and work, into the Christian message and to derive it from him, was long ago condemned by the church as heresy. In the patristic period, the suggestion that Jesus' humanity was phantasmal, that the heavenly being, Christ, was but acting out a part as a human and merely seeming to have flesh and blood, was seen as destructive of authentic Christianity. It is this same tendency that Barth, Cullmann and Jeremias, to mention only a few of the critics, have seen reappearing in Bultmann's thought. Likewise, Tillich's other proposal that Jesus grew into divinity was also proposed and as firmly opposed in the early church. This inverts the biblical order, supposing that the flesh became Word rather than the Word becoming flesh. The doctrine of incarnation becomes in Tillich's thought merely one of inspiration. God does not reach down to man but man reaches up to God. Oppose liberalism as he will, Tillich's true parentage still shows through in these inversions.

Once a true incarnation has been yielded, it becomes difficult, even if it is desirable, to put any unique significance into Jesus' death. Barth has wondered whether John the Baptist's execution could serve as well as Jesus' in Bultmann's thought, for both are images of death and there is no intrinsic reason why the one should not induce self-understanding as much as the other. The same, of course, could also be argued for Dietrich Bonhoeffer who could easily be seen as a more contemporary 'Christ-figure'.

Bultmann speaks of Christianity being unique but he refuses to yoke its contents to empirical history. The reason for this, Barth suggests, is his 'superstition' that only what can be scientifically proved can be regarded as historical. And Bultmann will not allow that history is ever other than subjective. We cannot detach ourselves from it, he says, as we do from nature which we observe. Such a narrow, eccentric definition virtually destroys all historical work, whether religious or secular.

The truth of the matter is that there are masses of events which occur each day for which later 'scientific proof' is impossible. The absence of demonstrable proof, however, in no way invalidates the fact that the events took place. In the case of the New Testament, it is remarkable to note that as historians of Greco-Roman civilization have been growing in confidence about what can be known about Jesus' contemporaries from sources far inferior to those Christians possess, Bultmann and his disciples have reached total scepticism about Jesus. This scepticism, it would appear, arises not from the historical data as from a philosophical predisposition.

Bultmann's programme of demythologization and Tillich's use of religious symbols have both been criticized severely. It is important to note that no other literature is ever treated in this way and those in other fields are often mystified as to how demythologizers reach their conclusions. C. S. Lewis, who was not without some skill in these matters, asked of Bultmann, 'Through what strange process has this learned German gone in order to make himself blind to what all men expect to see? ... It is Bultmann *contra mundum*.'[38]

Demythologization, says Ridderbos, 'plays havoc with the very heart of the New Testament message', because as soon as God's activity within history and especially in the man Jesus is discarded as 'myth', of necessity God becomes remote, distant, obscured, cut off from the world.[39] It is a device which has ramifications for all parts of the Christian faith. But is this hermeneutical device justified?

Bultmann's point of departure is the assumption that the New

Testament writers shared his own existential approach to personal existence which, in turn, can be extracted from the mythological garb in which it is concealed. It may be questioned that this was actually the case and the fact that Bultmann thinks that it is may be nothing more than another instance of someone looking down the long well of human history and seeing his own face reflected at the bottom.

To scrap the mythological garb is, in fact, to evacuate Christianity of its saving content. For what is discarded is not, as Bultmann imagines, secondary and peripheral but primary and central. What he makes accessible to the modern mind with its naturalistic and secular caste is no longer biblical faith. He avoids the seeming 'foolishness' of a spatio-temporal cross but ends up with one which is nothing more than a personal insight. Paul, he acknowledges, expounded the atonement in penal and classic terms; he himself opts for the mystical, subjective theory.

Tillich's use of symbol in religious language has also been subjected to criticism. It is by no means clear how the word-symbol participates in the reality it represents as, Tillich says, fire does in the smoke which it generates. This is clearly what lies behind his insistence that Christian word-symbols such as 'Christ' are necessary, rather than arbitrary. They are not, he insists, free creations. Yet it is not clear why they could not be. After all, having disavowed belief in the traditional Trinity as well as in an historic incarnation, he goes on to posit that Jesus grew into divinity. 'Christ' therefore becomes a 'symbol' of the union between God and man which Jesus pioneered. But could we not find other symbols which could as well point to this union? Why should we utilize 'Christ' rather than 'Mahatma Gandhi' or 'Buddha'? The choice would seem to be a trifle arbitrary.

Both the strength and the weakness of the existential theology is its attempt to become relevant to the modern mind. The problem is that it has demythologized the New Testament rather than the modern mind. Where the biblical outlook violates the assumptions of modern man it is these assumptions which need to be depicted as mythological. This, in fact, is what Scripture itself does. The profane person could argue that history is but a tissue of natural cause and effect, but the biblical authors countered that it was also the arena of God's providential activity. The fact that this person was unable to recognize the hand of God in human affairs indicated that he was in bondage to a mythological world-view from which he needed to be redeemed. The Egyptians, looking only for natural cause and effect, might explain the parting of the sea or the prevalence of plagues naturalistically, but God's people knew differently. Nebuchadnezzar might destroy Israel for his own reasons but the prophet sees him merely as a tool in God's hand. Judas, calculating shrewdly, might give up his master, but it was the Father in and through this act who delivered up the Son and the Son who delivered up himself. Man in rebellion has always sought to exclude God from this world, and it does him no service if Christian theologians write their soteriologies to conform to, rather than to challenge, this rebellion.

It is certainly inadequate to interpret 'condemnation' and divine 'wrath' simply as man's inner sense of alienation as Tillich does. To do so is not merely to deny the external, divine reality and to refuse to know what can be known about God, but it is to lead Christianity down a strange path. As Ladd has pointed out, the existential theologies fly in the face of almost two thousand years of Christian consensus as to what the faith is all about. 'If salvation is correctly understood in terms of authentic existence; if authenticity means complete independence of all external securities, including objective acts of God in history and objectifying theological statements about God, man, and salvation; then it is difficult to see how any one prior to the emergence of existentialism can properly be called Christian.'[40] It is possible that Bultmann and Tillich have the true gospel and millions of 'uncritical believers' in all ages have had only a perversion of it. The chances of this being the case, however, are infinitesimally small.

Notes

[1] Further explanation of these terms can be found in Norman Perrin, *The Promise of Bultmann* (Philadelphia, 1969), pp. 37–45.

[2] What is said of Bultmann could also be said of Tillich. 'His *Systematic Theology* represents the summation of his life's work. It is conceived as an *apologetic* theology in conscious opposition to the kerygmatic theology which Karl Barth holds to be the true type of Christian Theology.' Kenneth Hamilton, 'Paul Tillich', *Creative Minds in Contemporary Theology*, ed. Philip Edgcumbe Hughes (Grand Rapids, 1966), p. 454.

[3] Bultmann acknowledges the 'decisive influence' Heidegger has had on his thought; in Heidegger, he says, he found a 'conceptuality' capable of interpreting existence adequately. See

his 'Autobiographical Reflections', *Existence and Faith: Shorter Writings of Rudolf Bultmann*, ed. Schubert M. Ogden (New York, 1960: London, 1961), p. 288.

⁴ Tillich tends to blur the distinction between object and subject in the work of doing history; this, of course, is seen as necessary and it is what, in the area of New Testament exegesis, constitutes the 'new hermeneutic'. His *Perspectives on Nineteenth and Twentieth Century Protestant Theology* is so full of personal reminiscences that Claude Welch has suggested that it would be kinder to Tillich not to mention the book at all. It also exhibits an unfortunate German parochialism, for it has omitted any discussion at all on British and American theologians in this period.

⁵ See John B. Cobb, *Living Options in Protestant Theology: A Survey of Methods* (Philadelphia, 1962), pp. 199–226.

⁶ In one of his better-known judgments, Bultmann declares: 'I do indeed think that we can now know almost nothing concerning the life and personality of Jesus, since the early Christian sources show no interest in either, are moreover fragmentary and often legendary; and other sources about Jesus do not exist.' Rudolf Bultmann, *Jesus and the Word* (London, 1934: New York, 1958), p. 8. The same position is sustained in his *History of the Synoptic Tradition* (Oxford and New York, 1963).

⁷ Joachim Jeremias, 'The Present Position in the Controversy Concerning the Problem of the Historical Jesus', *Expository Times,* 69 (August 1958), p. 335.

⁸ Paul Tillich, *Systematic Theology* (3 vols.; Chicago, 1951–63: London, 1951–64), II, p. 102.

⁹ *Ibid.,* p. 97.

¹⁰ *Ibid.,* p. 109.

¹¹ Bultmann's use of the word 'myth' is complex and at times obscure. The problems are well aired in John Macquarrie, *The Scope of Demythologizing: Bultmann and his Critics* (London, 1960) and the rebuttal of Macquarrie's conclusions in Schubert M. Ogden, *Christ Without Myth: A Study Based on the Theology of Rudolf Bultmann* (New York, 1961), pp. 165–181 and 95–126. Bultmann first broached the subject in a pamphlet in 1941, *Offenbarung und Heilsgeschehen*. This, together with numerous responses to it, may be found in Hans Werner Bartsch, ed., *Kerygma and Myth: A Theological Debate* (2 vols.; London, 1964). Not all of the German edition of Bartsch, however, has been translated into English.

¹² The only statement that is not symbolic for Tillich is that God is being-itself (Tillich, *Systematic Theology,* I, p. 239). This means that God is not one being among others. As soon as we begin to conceptualize this power we necessarily use symbols and images drawn from earthly, finite existence. These always misrepresent what God is; to that extent they are verbal idols. The God who is being-itself is always beyond and behind our verbal conceptualizations, the cumulative result of which we impudently call 'God'.

¹³ Philip Edgecumbe Hughes, *Scripture and Myth: An Examination of Rudolf Bultmann's Plea for Demythologization* (London, 1956), p. 5.

¹⁴ Rudolf Bultmann, *Theology of the New Testament* (2 vols.; New York, 1951–55), I, pp. 32, 226, 227.

¹⁵ *Ibid.,* I, p. 227.

¹⁶ *Ibid.,* I, p. 270.

¹⁷ Throughout Bultmann's *Theology* the translator has taken the liberty of translating the Greek and German words for 'justification' as 'rightwise' or being 'rightwised'. The word he has employed is an old Middle English one which he himself calls 'obsolete'. Given this fact, it is difficult to see how this translation meshes with contemporary consciousness.

¹⁸ Bultmann, *Theology,* I, pp. 284, 285.

¹⁹ *Ibid.,* pp. 297, 298.

²⁰ *Ibid.,* p. 300.

[21] *Ibid.*, p. 306.

[22] See K. E. Logstrup, 'The Doctrines of God and Man in the Theology of Rudolf Bultmann', *The Theology of Rudolf Bultmann*, ed. Charles W. Kegley (New York, 1966), pp.83–96.

[23] John Macquarrie, *An Existential Theology: A Comparison of Heidegger and Bultmann* (London and New York, 1955), pp. 154, 155.

[24] Rudolf Bultmann, *Essays, Philosophical and Theological* (London, 1955), p. 85.

[25] Bultmann, *Theology*, I, p. 307.

[26] Oscar Cullman, 'Rudolf Bultmann's Concept of Myth and the New Testament', *Concordia Theological Monthly*, 27, No. 1 (January 1956), p. 18.

[27] Barth's study, *Rudolf Bultmann: Ein Versuch ihn zu Verstehen* (Zollikon – Zürich, 1952), deals incisively with Bultmann's whole position, but some of the criticisms depend, of course, on the validity of Barth's own objective concerns.

[28] Bultmann's argument against miracles understood as a breach in the uniformity of cause and effect is essentially Humean. It is answered in C. S. Lewis, *Miracles: A Preliminary Study* (London and New York, 1947), pp. 103–111.

[29] Paul S. Minear, 'Rudolf Bultmann's Interpretation of New Testament Eschatology', *The Theology of Rudolf Bultmann*, p. 73.

[30] Tillich, *Systematic Theology*, II, p. 166.

[31] *Ibid.*, pp. 44, 45.

[32] Tillich was deeply moved by his experience of Buddhism and other oriental religions, an account of which is given in his *Christianity and the Encounter of the World Religions*. In his last public lecture, 'The Significance of the History of Religions for the Systematic Theologian', he declared that had time permitted he would have rewritten his *Systematic Theology* in terms of these non-Christian religions. Charles Hartshorne's essay, 'Tillich's Doctrine of God' and Reinhold Niebuhr's 'Biblical Thought and Ontological Speculation in Tillich's Theology' are illuminating in this respect. See Charles W. Kegley and Robert W. Bretall, eds., *The Theology of Paul Tillich* (New York, 1952), pp. 164–197, 216–229.

[33] Tillich, *Systematic Theology*, II, p. 177.

[34] Ralph Martin, 'The New Quest of the Historical Jesus', *Jesus of Nazareth: Saviour and Lord*, ed. Carl F. H. Henry (Grand Rapids, 1966), p. 39. The same conclusion is reached by Graham Stanton in his meticulous analysis, *Jesus of Nazareth in New Testament Preaching* (London, 1974).

[35] Paul Althaus, *Fact and Faith in the Kerygma of Today* (Philadelphia, 1959), p. 82.

[36] Paul Edwards, 'Professor Tillich's Confusions', *Mind*, 74 (1965), p. 197.

[37] The important essay on 'Gnosis' in Kittel's *Wörterbuch* was, of course, provided by Bultmann and subsequently published separately as *Gnosis* (London, 1952). He has not conceded that the recent findings of gnostic texts have in any way invalidated his position. That there was a gnostic movement, as opposed to general influences such as oriental theosophy and Greek philosophy which antedated the New Testament period, has been asserted but not established. All of the gnostic writings that have been found are post-Christian. This puts in jeopardy Bultmann's claim that Paul's thought is in part borrowed from that of the gnostics. On the general subject, see Edwin M. Yamauchi, *Pre-Christian Gnosticism: A Survey of the Proposed Evidences* (Grand Rapids, 1970: London, 1973).

[38] C. S. Lewis, *Christian Reflections* (Grand Rapids, 1967), p. 156.

[39] See Hermann Ridderbos, *Bultmann* (Philadelphia, 1960), pp. 23–36.

[40] George Eldon Ladd, *Rudolf Bultmann* (Chicago, 1964), p. 39.

The more that man posits in God, the less he retains for himself.

Karl Marx

Atheism is humanism.

Jean-Paul Sartre

The Gods have fled. The world has become man's task and man's responsibility.

Harvey Cox

A God without wrath brought men without sin into a kingdom without judgment through the ministration of a Christ without a cross.

H. Richard Niebuhr

Chapter Four

God in a Godless world

The Reformation produced its own culture, its own views of art, government, and human relations; so, too, did the Enlightenment. Until recently these two systems had seemed to be rivals, the one centring on God and his Christ and the other on man and his reason. The extent to which the one was embraced was the extent to which the other had to be rejected.

During the last few years, however, this assessment of the options has been challenged by several radical theologies. The point at issue is the relationship of the Enlightenment's secularism to the purposes of God. Formerly secularism and its accompanying humanism were seen by those in the Reformation tradition as expressions of man's rebellion against God; now, it is proposed, they might be seen as indications of God's active involvement in the world. The issue simply is whether secularism is a token of sin or a sign of salvation. Is it, therefore, something to be challenged, or something to be accepted and nurtured?

Definition of secularism

What is secularism, how has it come about and what are its tangible workings? As used today, the word *secularism*[1] is a synonym for naturalism, and whether this is considered a good or a bad thing will depend, of course, on which of these interpretations is accepted. It is a presupposition, or functional attitude, that the empirical world is alone real and that every effort to give its events transcendent meaning should be abandoned.

We can put this another way by saying that modern man's self-identity as a religious being is under siege. When this assault began and what its precise nature is have been debated. Sigmund Freud, however, believed that in the late nineteenth century, western man was suffering from three 'wounds'. The first, Freud argued, had been struck by Copernicus who removed man from the centre of the universe and relegated him instead to a wandering constellation in a universe having neither centre nor periphery, whose edges run out into eternal silence. The second wounding blow was delivered by Darwin who undermined man's sense of importance, not cosmologically, but biologically. Man came to see himself as merely one part of life's processes, neither separate from them nor elevated over them. It should be added, too, that the sense of purpose in life provided by an understanding of divine providence was often destroyed by the idea of 'natural selection', a weening process in a mindless system cruelly 'red in tooth and claw'. Routed from the natural world, nineteenth-century people found little refuge in the Bible; it, too, was under assault. Biblical criticism seemed to have demolished any hope of discovering a transcendent Word in the wreckage of the text, and the twentieth century has not reversed this substantially.[2] And even where there is an effort to come to terms with it as revelation, common agreement as to its meaning is hampered by serious hermeneutical questions. While some insist that Scripture speaks with different voices, others argue that different ears inevitably hear different things. The third 'wound' to which Freud called attention was delivered through his own work. He believed that he had shown that man's vaunted rational powers by which systems of thought are erected, values defined and meaning derived are merely dancing to the tune piped by dark, uncharted, subterranean instincts.[3]

As commonly summarized, this trend in the modern period has produced an overwhelming sense that God is very elusive or, perhaps, not there at all, that man is alone and uncared-for in this world, that absolutes are part of a discredited effort to impose meaning on the cruel and chaotic events of life, that this should now be abandoned, and that if meaning is to be found it will not come through appealing to external authorities but will be found only in the analysis of man's self-experience.[4] This is the cultural *Geist* in which modern man lives and in which all theology must function either by way of attraction or rejection.

It does not follow, of course, that the expression of secularism will take the same form or will be developed with the same intensity in all of the western countries. Martin Marty rightly points out that in fact the continental European countries have given secularism its most forceful expression, that this is somewhat modified in Britain and that it is modified somewhat further in America, what he distinguishes respectively as 'utter', 'mere' and 'controlled' secularism.[5] Different as these may be in the degree of their thoroughness, they nevertheless rest on common assumptions. There is a recognizable secular life-style in all of these countries.

The secular man in the street probably gives no allegiance to any central 'philosophy' by which he evaluates life. The growing complexities of modern society have made him suspicious of those with sure answers to its problems. Those who are most abreast of the modern world, he observes, are often those who demur most firmly from embracing any one ideology or set of values. However bigoted this man may be racially, however ignorant educationally, however crippled psychologically, he likes to think of himself as being 'open-minded' philosophically, moving amphibiously from thought-world to thought-world if need be. He is uninterested in fixed principles, closed systems, transcendent ideals or enduring philosophical commitments.

To a large extent this modern, post-literate man is non-reflective, the more so if he is a TV addict, as he probably is. He is content merely to survive the common events of everyday life and, as much as possible, he would like to be spared the pain of having to think about them. His success he measures by the pay he earns, the satisfaction he receives, the domestic tranquillity he enjoys, the friends he makes, the pleasure he manufactures and the security he negotiates. It matters little to him if Marxism is regnant in the world or Eastern gurus sell their wares in his own town provided the Gross National Product goes up, his own life is bettered, his personal grievances are alleviated, his leisure time expanded and his freedoms – perhaps even including the freedom from responsibility – are enlarged.[6]

Given this mindset, it is not difficult to see that his understanding of Christian salvation could be rather minimal. He might even equate it with fulfilment or success.[7] He may believe that these are really three different ways of looking at the same thing, the first religious, the second psychological and the third pragmatic. For the cultural framework in which our religious terms are frequently interpreted empties them of their meaning, at least in any historic sense. These terms assume the existence of a higher order, a transcendent world, a triune God in whom the visible world subsists; our culture assumes that beneath and behind the social fabric there is no meaningful world or higher order.[8] Van Buren therefore contends that 'the juxtaposition of his [the Christian's] faith, expressed in traditional terms, and his ordinary way of thinking [which Van Buren thinks is secular], causes a spiritual schizophrenia'.[9] No one, Bultmann remarked caustically, who uses electricity can still believe – at least in the old way.

Secularism enters theology

The inescapable reality of secularism has forced theologians to make some hard choices. Either Christian faith can be presented as an alternative to secularism, or secularism can be seen as an expression of Christian faith. Theologies which choose the latter, working within secular assumptions, will want to express the autonomy of the world from God as traditionally conceived, admit that truth is relative, eschew absolutes, dismiss metaphysical considerations, and will work to evolve a life-view from within human experience, rather than from some exterior source. By contrast, theologies offering an alternative to secularism will insist on the existence of a transcendent reality which nevertheless undergirds the fabric of our social life, that the purposes of God are governed by moral concerns which reflect his holiness, that meaning and purpose in life are found in terms of these absolute purposes, that the failure to do so results in social and moral decay, the end result of which is guilt, derangement and dysfunction, and that God alone has the love and power to reverse these calamities through Christ.

The presence of a secular outlook provides an ideal environment for the emergence of humanism.[10] Indeed, Karl Marx argued that it was not possible to affirm man without denying God, but in those Christian theologies which believe God is affirmed as and when man is, the operating assumptions are still secular. But if God exists, he certainly does not do so in terms of classic theism. Consequently, those theologies which have opted to allow secular presuppositions have inevitably become humanistic.

The intrusion of this humanism into Christian theology has been charted by Roger Shinn,[11] using two symbolic points of reference as a measuring rod. These are the Oxford Conference on Church, Community and State (1937) and the Geneva Conference on Church and Society (1966) of the WCC. The former, recognizing the latent dangers of German nationalism, spoke somberly of the burdens and oppressions of modern society. It acknowledged that Christianity had become so much like the world around it that it had lost the right to ask the world to become like itself. There was, in other words, still a large sense of antithesis that was felt to exist between Christianity and secularism. At Geneva, thirty years later, the former pessimism was replaced by a new optimism and a loss of this antithesis. There was an emphasis on human 'dignity' as formerly there had been on human depravity. The word *humanism* was heard again and again, but it was a religious humanism of which they were speaking. The theological element was introduced through the thought of God's immersion in secular processes and his solidarity with man through Jesus Christ. 'The human is the measure of all things, because God became human in Jesus Christ,'[12] declared one delegate. The Christian mission, therefore, came to be seen primarily as the 'humanizing' of institutions, and the great foe of Christian faith was seen as all of those developments in our urbanized, modern, technological society which dehumanize people.[13] It is this perception of things which provides the context against which the theologies in this chapter must be understood.

A similar development has, of course, occurred on the Catholic side as well. At first Protestant and Catholic thinkers tended to work separately and therefore the new attempts at uniting Christian faith in terms of secular reality moved merely along parallel lines. During the last decade, however, the traditions have merged, with significant interaction between Catholic and Protestant theologians taking place.

Teilhard de Chardin and Walter Ong, for example, have seen the 'shaking of the foundations' as evidence that God is actually active within our electronic age. Even Pope John XXIII, in his opening address to the Second Vatican Council, gently mocked the 'prophets of gloom' who, he said, 'are always forecasting disaster, as though the end of the world were at hand'. By contrast, he went on to share his belief that in 'the present order of things, Divine Providence is leading us to a new order of human relations which, by men's own efforts and even beyond their very expectations, are directed toward the fulfilment of God's superior and inscrutable designs'.[14] This line of thought has subsequently been developed under the rubric of 'hominization', the thought being that man is now reaching the fullness of his own capabilities and assuming control over his planet; this is his God-given destiny and what the Christian doctrine of eschatology is all about. Needless to say, it is also what humanism is about, too.

This new direction in Christian thought was pioneered on its Protestant side, largely by Bonhoeffer during the last year of his life.[15] Given the pervasiveness of secularity, how should modern man be viewed? To argue, as conservative evangelicals have, that modern man is essentially the same in nature as ancient man, summoned in the same way to repentance and belief in Christ through the gospel, seemed to Bonhoeffer to be an abdication from responsibility. Nor was he entirely content with Tillich's view that modern man is asking religious questions in non-religious and sometimes irreligious ways. Bonhoeffer's starting point, instead, was that man is now beyond religion altogether and it is at this point that theology must start its work.

The premise of Bonhoeffer's mature theology, then, was that the world has 'come of age'.[16] By this he did not mean that it had reached a utopian threshold of moral purity. That would have been hard to maintain as he languished in a Nazi prison. Rather, he meant that it has come to a place of independent maturity in much the same way as a child does eventually. From one point of view, then, secularism (a term which Bonhoeffer disliked) may seem like human rebellion against God, but from another it can be seen as God's process of educating man, that process by which he is brought to adulthood. If this is so, then God is obviously working with men outside of the circles of organized religion, meeting them incognito. Recognizing this is to see 'true worldliness' and here, among the seemingly irreligious, is 'unconscious Christianity'. Not only are the forms of institutional religion unnecessary to this latent Christianity but they are impediments to it.[17]

Consonant with this, Bonhoeffer developed a strong opposition to the personal and inward aspect of Christian faith. This he saw as the last stage of religion which needed to be overcome. He scoffed at the notion of private sins, such as the sexual infidelities of Napoleon and Goethe, and argued that it was never a pastor's duty to preach against or 'pry' into these; to do so, he said, would be to become trapped within 'methodism'. Nor, indeed, should the pastor attempt to show that Christ is the 'answer' for inevitably this will lead him to exaggerate the personal shortcomings of the congregation and this will be done only out of the fear that the church will be engulfed by secularism and will cease to have a role in modern life. Thus he boldly declared:

The attack by Christian apologetic upon the adulthood of the world I consider to be in the first place pointless, in the second ignoble, and in the third un-Christian. Pointless, because it looks to me like an attempt to put a grown man back into adolescence, i.e. to make him dependent on things on which he is not in fact dependent any more, thrusting him back into the midst of problems which are in fact not problems for him any more. Ignoble, because this amounts to an effort to exploit the weakness of man for purposes alien to him and not freely subscribed to by him. Un-Christian, because for Christ himself is being substituted one particular stage in the religiousness of man, i.e. a human law.[18]

Secularism, therefore, should not be seen as a perversion but as part of man's divinely ordained maturation. Christ is not exiled from our irreligious world but is present in it. He confronts people, not in the old process of repentance, faith, conversion, regeneration and sanctification, but in new ways through their 'godless' attitudes. Then, people needed the church; now, they do not. The old ways of thinking, consequently, need to be destroyed. We must learn to put the biblical concepts into non-religious language which the secular person will readily grasp and which will be compatible with his own experience of being emancipated by God from religion.[19] To be a Christian, he said, did not mean being religious, but 'being a man'. It is, in other words, to celebrate the 'emancipation' which humanism announces but to see this as the gracious, unmerited work of God.

Bonhoeffer's fragmentary prison writings, which can hardly be said to provide the main lines of a major theology, nevertheless had an extraordinarily seminal effect. Tantalized by his proposals, scholars set to work evolving a theological response to secularism, encouragement for this being provided in 1959 by the Consultation held at the

Ecumenical Institute, Bossey, Switzerland, the subject being 'The Meaning of the Secular'.

There is no simple way to chart the results of this work. First of all, there is constant overlapping between the several different 'schools' of thought. Secondly, it is an exaggeration to speak of these efforts as theologies since their development has not been pursued with great profundity or thoroughness. Indeed, in passing from the era of Barth, Brunner, Bultmann and Tillich to that of Robinson, Cox and Altizer, one is moving into a different world and one which is noticeably insubstantial in comparison. Thirdly, in the last two decades, interest in soteriology has waned considerably outside of evangelical circles and this has made it difficult to provide cogent summaries.

Broadly speaking, those concerned to fashion a response to secularism fell into two schools. First, there were those like Harvey Cox and Friedrich Gogarten who have developed their thought along sociological lines. Salvation was sought in and equated with social and political change. Secondly, there were the radicals whose emphases differed a little depending on whether they were British or American. In Britain this school was comprised of John Robinson, Ronald Gregor Smith, John Wren Lewis, Werner and Lotte Pelz and Daniel Jenkins. In North America, this radicalism was articulated by the death-of-God theologians, namely, Gabriel Vahanian, William Hamilton, Paul van Buren and Thomas Altizer. It soon became clear, however, that there were sharp differences among them. As a 'soft' radical, Vahanian believed only in the perishing of traditional theistic ideas[20] whereas the others, 'hard' radicals, thought also that God had either passed into another form of existence or ceased to be altogether. It is in the recognition of this fact that salvation consists.

These radical theologies were, in a way, nourished on Barthian ideas.[21] Barth had refused to speak of God in a secular way, but he nevertheless did utilize a secular understanding of the world. History and nature were viewed naturalistically even if God was not. These two orders, the visible and invisible, rested precariously on one another, their mutual relation flimsy to say the least, interconnected only at intervals by divine 'mighty acts' or by the slicing of the divine Word into human experience. In liberalism, the 'supernatural' was contained within the natural; in Barthianism, it was sundered from the natural almost completely. This relationship between the orders

104

showed up most sharply in Barth's notion of *Historie* and *Geschichte*. There were irreconcilable tensions within this idea. Bultmann exploited the instability in one direction, arguing for *Geschichte* without *Historie*; the new theologies argued in the other direction that one could have *Historie* (now understood as the warp and woof of secularized life) without *Geschichte* (transcendent, divine meaning). Caught in this scissor action, Barthianism rapidly declined as a serious theological option.

The relationship between the American and British theologies is difficult to pinpoint and it is probably wiser to treat them as parallel and largely independent tendencies. There are differences between them. Cox, for example, sought God in that kind of social change in which injustice is being overcome and he argued that interest in the personal dimension of faith can be pursued only at the price of the societal. By contrast, Robinson argued that the key to Christian faith is the discovery of and growing openness to the 'ground' of one's being. His interest in societal matters was not very marked although he believed that the gracious God is found in the gracious neighbour. Van Buren, by a ruthless application of linguistic analysis, eliminated all meaningful 'God talk'; Robinson, meanwhile, was launched into his exploration of God, positing a panentheism in which everything was in God and God was in everything. Van Buren was atheistic; Robinson, like Spinoza before him, was 'God-intoxicated' although Alistair McIntyre countered rightly that this, too, could be seen as atheism when judged by Christian standards. Cox was critical of the death-of-God theologians, although he was favourably impressed by their emasculated christology. His interests are sociological and urban, rather than metaphysical, and Marty is probably right in saying that he should be classified simply as a 'Baptist utopian-visionary' rather than as an iconoclastic atheist. Despite their differences, however, there were important points of agreement between the radicals, and these will be explored, using Cox, Robinson and Altizer as general representatives.

The supernatural dismissed

First, each one was agreed that the familiar distinction in 'classical theism' between the natural and supernatural is no longer credible to modern man and must be abolished.[22] Robinson parodied this idea in terms of a three-decker bus and suggested that the spatial image was once taken seriously. God was thought to be 'up there'. In time the crudity of this was modified so that God was merely 'out there', but further purification is still necessary.[23] Cox put the matter differently, saying that we have moved from an ontological to a functional way of speaking of God, from a gaseous and diffuse philosophizing to a concrete recognition of God as identified with sociological change. Altizer's argument was even more dramatic. God as transcendent was an oppressive and satanic tyrant, but he has passed out of this form of existence to enter our world and become immanent in it. In Jesus, therefore, God died.[24]

Altizer and Robinson both used the Tillichian idea of God as the 'ground' of our being.[25] God is not a person distinct from and over against ourselves, but rather is identical with our deepest experiences, the mystical perceptions and moral intuitions that we have. Becoming 'open' to this reality is what salvation is about, but in the nature of the case this is not a uniquely Christian experience. Cox, however, eschewed the mystical-existential understanding and suggested that God is found where the poor are treated with respect, injustice is overturned and dehumanization is replaced by compassion.[26] The result of this type of theism is that many of the antitheses upon which the biblical gospel depends had now vanished, such as those between Creator and creation, eternity and time, absolute and relative, good and evil, salvation and judgment.[27]

Christ redefined

Secondly, the inevitable consequence of this new theistic basis for Christian faith was a christology largely evacuated of the divine element. Robinson at first explored this meagerly, being content simply to see Jesus as the man for others.[28] Cox, however, stated flatly that the historical facts of Jesus' life are incompatible 'with the catalogue of divine attributes listed in most forms of theism'. He went on to say that we are therefore forced to choose 'whether we must begin with theistic premises and somehow fit Christ in, or begin with Christ and see what happens'.[29] He opted for the latter course, claiming that 'the gospel must oppose (traditional) theism as such as atheism'. Altizer likewise pursued this notion ending up with a radical, kenotic view in which God abandoned not merely the relative attributes – omnipresence, omniscience, omnipotence – in order to be incarnate but all of his attributes, passing out of one form of existence and into another.

The issue which they raised is undoubtedly a difficult one, for the limited nature of all humanity, including that of Jesus, seems incompatible with the unlimited nature of God. From one point of view, Jesus as God should have known everything; from the other point of view, Jesus as man could not and did not know everything. As God, Jesus should have been omnipresent, whereas as authentically human he could not have been everywhere. As God, his power was without limits, but as man he suffered from weakness. It is no surprise that these difficulties in the Chalcedonian two-nature doctrine have once again surfaced; what is surprising is that Cox and Altizer almost leave one with the impression that they were the first to see the difficulty and that their quick and easy solution should lay the whole matter to rest.

In the more profound statements of kenoticism there is an element of authentic concern. For the christologies produced during the period of Protestant scholasticism almost had God masquerading as a human. The humanity of Christ was very pale indeed. In reaction to this, some scholars began to emphasize the matter of human psychology, his growth and development as a person. If he was fully human, then he did not arrive in the world with an adult perception of things but rather, as the Scripture affirms, he grew in stature and wisdom. If his knowledge was expanding, then he could not have been omniscient. Consequently Philippians 2:5–11 came to have great importance in the discussion, it being assumed that the phrase 'he emptied himself' (verse 7) meant that he abandoned the relative attributes in order to be incarnate. Some writers went even further and proposed that his entire self-consciousness as the second person of the Godhead was extinguished and that it was only near the end of his life that he grew back into it. Altizer, with apparently little knowledge of the voluminous discussions that have swirled around this subject in the past, has gone a step further in saying that Christ's divine existence was extinguished and that it will never be recovered.

The concern with the reality of Jesus' humanity is as necessary as the matching concern for his divinity. Where the one is pursued at the price of the other, however, the author parts company with the apostolic witness as well as with Jesus himself. In no sense was the divine circuitry interrupted. The communication between Father, Son and Spirit was unbroken, and the incarnation cannot be interpreted in terms of a leave of absence on the part of the Son or, still worse, as the destruction of the Godhead.

Jesus' humanity can be preserved inviolate by positing that the Godhood lacked the relative attributes, but does that preserve the Godhood inviolate? By definition, a God who does not know everything, who is not everywhere and who is not all-powerful is not the God of biblical revelation. The solution proffered by the seventeenth-century Tübingen theologians is still worthy of consideration, namely that in the mystery of his personhood these attributes were hidden and only utilized on rare occasions. This seeks to explain both his ignorance as to the time of the parousia as well as the instances of undoubted prescience in his dealings with some people, as well as the extraordinary circumstances of the transfiguration. Given the fact that Altizer, Robinson and Cox all make such a lavish use of mystery themselves, it seems strange that a modest appeal to it, such as this is, should seem so offensive and so unacceptable to them.

Salvation reinterpreted

Thirdly, the specifically soteriological concerns were all significantly reinterpreted to accommodate these other alterations in Christian belief. Robinson's concern with evangelism was unquestioned, but it is not easy to see what content could be put into his 'evangel', for he was insistent that we never meet God as a Being separate from ourselves, that he is identical with our 'ultimate concern', that no-one is without such concern, and that the traditional ideas of sin, repentance, justification and faith are obsolete in our space age. God makes us live in the world, Robinson affirmed, stripped of our supernaturalistic 'God-hypothesis'.

In Altizer there was a more thorough reworking of soteriology even if it was carried out more idiosyncratically as well. He was a proponent, on his own terms, of the classic and mystic views of the 'atonement', and an avowed opponent of the Latin. For if man must see Christ as his sinbearer, he must ever be submissive to God's 'distant and alien authority' which is what constitutes man's bondage.[30] Rather, Christ was sacrificed to overcome God's separation from the world – infinite over against finite, absolute over against relative – but this sacrifice is not a stationary, historic event. That would imply that there is a fixed point, an absolute revelatory statement to which Christians can look. In fact, all is in motion with contemporary re-enactments of the cross going on regularly in our secular life.

The unique elements of Christian faith were, therefore, abandoned. Jesus cannot be thought of as Son of God, he did not bear man's sin at the cross, he did not rise from the dead[31] and will not return in glory at the world's culmination. Faith in his saving death is not only unnecessary but harmful. The separation between God and man is overcome, not by Jesus dying for man before God, but by the transcendent God dying in Jesus before men. Seeing this is what opens us to the depth of our own being, liberates and saves us. Justification, therefore, is not by faith as Luther taught, nor by doubt as Tillich supposed, but by *denial*, denial that God the transcendent exists any more. Altizer, consequently, had little difficulty in wedding his Christianity with Buddhism, overlooking their opposition to one another and seeing the same 'Christ' mystically present in both.[32]

The mystical-existential fascination common to Robinson and Altizer was absent in Cox, but the reworking of traditional ideas was, nevertheless, as far-reaching. Cox's soteriology revolved around two theses. First, he argued that secularization, which he believed can be distinguished from secularism, is man's coming of age. Its origin is divine, its form is that of urbanization,[33] and its outcome is a new set of human relations that demands the reciprocity that only spiritual adults can supply.[34] Secondly, the gospel is the good news of salvation, not the bad news of sin and condemnation; in other words, his premise was that man is forgiven already and that he is simply called to work out this fact more completely in a new set of social relations.

It follows from this that sin is not rebellion against God's authority and commands, but the failure or unwillingness to discern what he is doing in society. 'The grammar of the Gospel', he said, 'is not a categorical imperative; it first of all points to what *is* occurring, only secondarily does it call for a consequent change in attitude or action.'[35] What God is doing was interpreted in terms of sonship. Formerly man lived under bondage and tutelage, Scripture using the idea of law to convey this (Gal. 3:15–4:7), but now man has been liberated to live an adult life independent of the former 'religious and metaphysical supports'. This is 'unlocking the gate of the playpen and turning man loose in an open universe',[36] and understanding this is conversion. To be 'converted', however, one also needs to be redeemed or liberated. In the Bible, it is 'principalities and powers' who stand over against man threatening his life; in our age, these can be seen as the forces which determine us, 'genes, glands and early toilet training'.[37] The demons of the New Testament are our repressed feelings; Jesus' exorcism is to be translated as the removal of our cultural neuroses so that we can live 'clearheaded and productive ways of life'.[38] The belief in a transcendent and supernatural order was dismissed as an 'irresponsible dodge' that distracts us from caring about this world. And an appropriate care for this world is what evangelism is all about. Ministers and nuns picketing against racial injustice, for example, are our evangelists, for secular man is *par excellence* political and therefore political action must be placed above any spiritual dimension in the declaration of the gospel.[39]

Evaluation

Cox was not far wrong in saying that millions of words in criticism have been provoked by his book *The Secular City* and the same, of course, could also be said of Robinson and Altizer. Indeed, the more striking responses were soon gathered up into three 'debate' books.[40] What is interesting in the responses, however, is that many of them are written by Barthians or those influenced by Barthian motifs. Their reply, more or less consistently, was that these thinkers had 'gone too far', Altizer in particular lending himself to sarcasm in this regard. The outrage, however, concealed some of the serious flaws in the Barthian outlook itself which these thinkers had exposed. The avalanche of criticism which fell on them is not, then, uniformly helpful in trying to get to the heart of the problem.

The chief merits of the radical theologies can be registered in three areas. First, they did exhibit the tensions within the Barthian system. Barth's massive theological synthesis included themes that were simply incompatible and flew apart once his dominating personality was no longer present to hold them together. It is to the credit of the radical theologians that they perceived that this system was not serviceable as it stood. Secondly, there was a candour in their writing which was refreshing because in theological circles it is all too rare. Thirdly, these theologies made a considerable effort to understand modern man, and it needs to be said of Cox in particular that his deep and genuine social concern is not a virtue to be dismissed too lightly. On the other side of the ledger, however, are some serious debits.

First, in all these schemes the Christian idea of God as the creator, preserver and sovereign Lord of all that there is was forfeited for a deity that bears no resemblance to the 'God and Father of our Lord Jesus Christ'. The impression we were given was that what was at issue was simply two different models, different word images, one of which made sense to secular people whereas the other did not. What was described as 'God', especially by Robinson and Altizer, however, was simply an extension of the human self. 'God', in their thought, was greater than but not separate from that self. This is not merely a different 'image' or model, but a different God. Writing of Robinson, J. I. Packer made this point, observing that

the choice that the bishop really offers us, whether intentionally or not, is not between two images of the same God, but between two Gods, two Christs, two histories, and ultimately two religions. The choice is between a God who is personal and a Father, and a God who is neither, but simply an aspect of ourselves; between a God who rules history, and speaks and acts in it, and a God who does not; between a pre-existent Saviour who was born of a virgin, bore a world's sin, rose from death, and will come again in glory, and a man named Jesus of whom none of these things was true; between a life of faith and fellowship with God, and a new sort of yoga. 'The faith which was once for all delivered unto the saints' is one thing, and Robinsonianism, as here expounded, is another.[41]

To those with any kind of theological memory at all, radical theology sounds altogether too familiar. Barth rightly chastised the Protestant liberals for imagining that they could call God by shouting 'man' in a loud voice, for what resulted as 'God' was simply a magnification of what man experienced himself to be; God, in other words, was cast in man's marred image and worshipped. That is idolatry.

Secondly, all three views rejected as unique God's revelation in Christ and in Scripture and then frequently they misunderstood those insights which they did accept as authentic. Jesus to them was not God incarnate, the only enfleshing of the true God, did not die for a world's sin, did not rise from the dead and will not return again. And each assumed that Scripture tells us less about God than about the authors who wrote it, that it is a record, not of divine disclosure, but of human discovery. The blurring of the 'divine' in Jesus and the relativizing of it in Scripture left these thinkers free to abandon Christian particularism on the one hand, and, on the other, to replace the teachings of the biblical Word by the insights of secular prophets and urban dwellers. The issue, therefore, is quite simple. Either Jesus was the incarnate God whose teachings, as recorded in Scripture, are enduringly true for every age; or his teachings are erroneous so that as modern secularized people we need to supplant or modify them by our own. What these thinkers appeared to have considered too little, however, was that their quick dismissal of the biblical preaching of the cross as 'irrelevant' for our age may be no different from its ancient dismissal as 'foolishness' (1 Cor. 1:18) for that of the Greeks, a charge made by those who are 'perishing'.

Thirdly, the loss of an ultimate antithesis between good and evil had serious ethical consequences. This loss was more pronounced in Altizer (who called God Satan) and Robinson (who saw God in everything and everything in God) than in Cox. All three, however, were universalists, and Robinson and Altizer embraced an ethical relativism guided only by an ill-defined and sentimental notion of love. The exception to this was Cox, who had some sharply defined ethical norms as these related to society. This was a fortunate inconsistency, for he had no base for maintaining an ethical system. Societal 'good', he equated with God's irruption within our secular processes, but he had to rely on his subjective perceptions – a 'discernment situation' – to decipher this aright. It was hardly a comfort to know, then, that by his own admission he had made numerous theological errors, because for the same reasons he probably made many errors in discerning whether or not it was God breaking out ethically in a particular situation.[42] Yet the fact that he did still have a structure of traditional ethics in which there was right and wrong meant that he could talk about sin, however misconstrued his talk was. In Robinson and

Altizer, there was virtually no mention of the subject.

Fourthly, the words connected with salvation – sin, faith, repentance, justification, conversion, atonement – were used, but in such a radically altered sense as to be unrecognizable to anyone familiar with New Testament discourse. This they saw as a virtue, since a scientifically oriented generation found it hard to comprehend what was meant by these words. It became a vice, however, when the reframing of the concepts progressed so far that the original content was no longer conveyed. The criticism, then, is not that they used different language but that they propagated a different gospel.

Finally, the implications for worship were deleterious.[43] Each author has admitted to his growing inability to 'get with' conventional devotional life and traditional worship. Even Cox admitted that whereas he once used to pray, now he only meditates. It certainly follows for Altizer and Robinson that worship was self-defeating, since it was merely the veneration of an extension of the self. Worship for God was worship for man since the being of God and the being of man are continuous. The secularism which was accepted so naively therefore spawned its true offspring, humanism.

These flaws would not have arisen if these authors had not misconstrued, first, the relationship of God to the world and, second, the nature of man. The 'God-hypothesis' was scrapped so that a new type of Christianity could be forged which was more compatible with secular assumptions. This was felt to be necessary because man is changing in his nature, and since he is far more sophisticated than his forebears, he needs to hear something different.

Cultural and technological changes there have been but to imagine that these have also changed man's nature is an assumption for which there is no supporting evidence; to imagine that they have changed man's nature for good, producing maturity and responsibility, is both naive and incredible. The twentieth century has witnessed more callous cruelty and inhumane destruction than any other before it. If we are to see in this, man 'come of age' with God's approval, then we might have grounds only to expect nothing other than a cosmic suicide in the future as he continues to 'age' and 'mature'.

Tailoring the biblical gospel to accommodate modern man, then, was hardly the striking radicalism that these authors imagined nor is it what modern man needs to hear. Far more radical and, as it turns out, serviceable in the cause of truth, are Packer's counter-propositions 'that the Bible is still right, that God is still on the throne, that the risen Christ is still mighty to save, that man remains the sinner he always was, that the apostolic gospel is still "the power of God unto salvation", and that not even such great mistakes as these we have been examining can finally stop its course, or thwart its triumph'.[44]

Notes

[1] *Secularism* is derived from *saeculum* meaning 'this present age'. It was used of the duration of one human generation or the length of a person's life. More generally, it connoted the 'spirit of the age'. It was basically, however, a time word for this world. It is tempting, therefore, to oppose it to the so-called Hebrew concept of the world which was more concrete. 'The whole history of Christian theology from the apologists of the second century onward can be understood in part as a continuing attempt to resist and dilute the radical Hebrew impulse, to absorb historical into spatial categories. . . . Only recently has the task of restoring the historical and temporal tenor to theology begun in earnest. The word *secular* was an early victim of the Greek unwillingness to accept the full brunt of Hebrew historicity.' Harvey Cox, *The Secular City: Secularization and Urbanization in Theological Perspective* (New York and London, 1965), pp. 32, 33. It may be doubted, however, whether Cox has sufficient reason for his dismissal of nearly two thousand years of Christian thought. He does this on the grounds that Hebrew and Greek concepts of the world were totally at odds with one another; that, it now seems clear, is a myth. See James Barr, *Old and New in Interpretation: A Study of the Two Testaments* (London, 1966), pp. 34–64.

[2] See Alan Richardson, *The Bible in the Age of Science* (London and Philadelphia, 1961); James Barr, *The Bible in the Modern World* (London, 1973). The state of the question is summarized by Barr in his 'The Authority of the Bible', *The Ecumenical Review*, XXI, No. 2 (April 1969), pp. 135–150.

[3] The process of secularization mentioned by Freud had to do with the unsettlement of the mind; there was a matching and additional unsettlement in society, 'mainly due to new machines, growth of big cities, massive transfer of populations'. See Owen Chadwick, *The Secularization of the European Mind in the Nineteenth Century* (Cambridge, 1975), pp. 161–249.

[4] The trend can be stated positively as 'the liberation of man from religious and metaphysical tutelage, the turning of his attention away from other worlds and towards this one'. Cox, *The Secular City*, p. 5 .

[5] Martin E. Marty, *The Modern Schism: Three Paths to the Secular* (London and New York, 1969).

[6] For a more extended analysis, see John Macquarrie, *New Directions in Theology Today*, III, *God and Secularity* (Philadelphia, 1967), pp. 45–58.

[7] R. A. Underwood, 'Essay on Religion in an Age of Science; Reflections upon the words "salvation", "fulfillment" and "success" ', *Zygon*, 2 (December 1967), pp. 331–364.

[8] That a major civilization is attempting, deliberately and self-consciously, to build without religious foundations is considered by some a unique event. Beneath all other civilizations, primitive or developed, there have always lain religious tenets of one sort or another and the social fabric has never been seen as an end in itself. This position was argued by Emil Brunner in

his *Christianity and Civilization* in a general way, defended specifically in his essay, 'Critic or Apologist of Civilization?', *Religion in Life*, XX, No. 3 (Summer 1951), pp. 323–337. *Cf.* Christopher Dawson, *The Historic Reality of Christian Culture: A Way to the Renewal of Christian Life* (London, 1960), pp. 79–98.

[9] Paul van Buren, *The Secular Meaning of the Gospel* (New York and London, 1963), p. 77. The same point is made brilliantly in Leonard Bernstein's *Mass* in which traditional Latin chants intermingle with rock and blues music, expressing the profound self-doubt and pain of modern man.

[10] It is as difficult to define *humanism* precisely as it is secularism. If it is agreed that the interests of God are displaced in favour of those of man or that those of God are interpreted through those of man, there is still a variety of expressions given to it ranging from Nietzsche's mysticism, through Comte's humanitarianism and into Marx's cold-eyed atheistic politics. Added to these forms are the various ways in which religious humanism has been expressed. What they all share in common, however, is the exclusion of the supernatural, confidence that man's rationality is sufficient to solve all human problems, morality based on experience, freedom of self-expression and the evolutionary nature of truth.

[11] Roger Lincoln Shinn, *New Directions in Theology Today*, VI, *Man: The New Humanism* (London and Philadelphia, 1968), pp. 19–25.

[12] *Ibid.*, p. 23.

[13] The pioneer of the notion of salvation as wholeness was Tillich. The word *salvation*, he argued, was derived from *salvus* meaning 'healing'. He saw the New Being arising from the healing of the breach between 'God' and man, man and his world, man and himself. See Tillich, *Systematic Theology*, II, pp. 165–167; and 'Relation of Religion and Health: Historical Considerations and Theoretical Questions', *Review of Religion*, X (May 1946), pp. 348–384; Wallace B. Clift, 'Tillich and Jung: A new mythology of "salvation"?' *Iliff Review*, XXXII, No. 1 (Winter 1975), pp. 3–15.

[14] Walter M. Abbott, *Documents of Vatican II* (London, 1967), pp. 712, 713.

[15] The interpretation of Bonhoeffer's thought has created difficulties. Many British scholars have sided with Barth in seeing his last phase as an enigmatic departure from the 'essential' Bonhoeffer who was conservatively neo-orthodox and is seen best in *The Cost of Discipleship*; radicals, such as Cox and Robinson, have seen his last thoughts as the climax, not the contradiction, anticipations of which are found in his earlier lectures on christology. The radicals, I believe, are correct. Hence Martin E. Marty's *The Place of Bonhoeffer* (London, 1963), is of less help in interpreting him than the brief essay in Eberhard Bethge, *Dietrich Bonhoeffer: Man of Vision, Man of Courage* (London and New York, 1970), pp. 757–795, which explicates the radical elements in Bonhoeffer's thought.

[16] Dietrich Bonhoeffer, *Letters and Papers from Prison* (London and New York, 1967), pp. 178–180.

[17] *Ibid.*, p. 152.

[18] *Ibid.*, p. 108.

[19] Barth's theology produced a strong antipathy to 'religion' in Europe. Religion was frequently interpreted in terms of *erōs*, man grasping after God to manipulate him. Barth, however, never believed that *agapē*, God's gracious intrusion into life, should be cut off from tangible religious forms; in his closing phase, Bonhoeffer did.

[20] *Cf.* John A. T. Robinson, 'Church and Theology; from here to where?' *Theology Today*, 25 (July 1968), pp. 149–168.

[21] The leaders of secular theology, Mascall notes, all had their first theological moorings in German Protestantism and represent the revolt from 'the extreme revelationism and supernaturalism of the school of Barth, Brunner and Heim'. Here is the violent swing 'from one extreme to the other, from a position which is all about God and grace to one which is all about man and

115

nature'. E. L. Mascall, *The Secularization of Christianity: An Analysis and Critique* (London, 1965), p. 120. It has seemed necessary to some to go beyond this statement, however. Bonhoeffer himself saw the seeds of secular theology to be lying implicitly in Barth's ideas and not merely by way of reaction. Certainly Barth's remarkable study, *The Humanity of God* (Richmond, 1960: London, 1967), gave encouragement to the new focus on man and nature. See Bonhoeffer, *Letters and Papers from Prison,* p. 120.

[22] It should be noted that other thinkers shared in the rejection of 'classical theism' with its distinction between natural and supernatural without embracing the radicals' solution. Most notable among these were the process theologians. See John B. A. Cobb, *A Christian Natural Theology: Based on the Thought of Alfred North Whitehead* (Philadelphia,1965: London, 1967); Bernard E. Meland, ed., *The Future of Empirical Theology* (Chicago, 1969); Leslie Dewart, *The Future of Belief: Theism In a World Come of Age* (New York, 1966: London, 1967); Schubert Ogden, *The Reality of God and Other Essays* (New York, 1966); Nelson Pike, *God and Timelessness* (New York and London, 1970); Norman W. Pittenger, *Process Thought and Christian Faith* (New York and London, 1968); *Christology Reconsidered* (London, 1970).

[23] Robinson made this a central issue in *Honest to God* (London and Philadelphia, 1963), pp. 29–44, but the same position is sustained in his *Exploration into God* (London and Stanford, 1967). See H. P. Owen, 'Later Theology of Dr J. A. T. Robinson', *Theology,* 72 (October 1970), pp. 449–455.

[24] Thomas J. J. Altizer, *The Gospel of Christian Atheism* (Philadelphia, 1966), pp. 102–131.

[25] Leon Morris in fact rightly contends that Robinson has sometimes *misused* Tillich's ideas, failing to see the strong religious motif that runs through Tillich's discussions of estrangement and the Ground of our being. See Morris's *The Abolition of Religion: A Study in 'Religionless Christianity'* (London, 1965), pp. 18–20.

[26] In opposition to the 'Hartford Appeal', Cox and some twenty other theologians penned the 'Boston Affirmations' in 1976. The activity of God, it was affirmed, can be seen in 'the struggles of the poor to gain a share of the world's wealth', in 'the transforming drive for ethnic dignity against the persistent racism of human hearts and social institutions', in 'the endeavor of women to overcome sexist subordination', in the efforts to overcome 'prideful domination and degrading passivity' in families, in the attempts to bring health care to the elderly, in the voices of those who resist the temptation 'to make a nation and its institutions objects of religious loyalty', in the concern of ecologists, in the work of scientists where religious issues are honoured, and in society where justice is done. *Cf.* Peter L. Berger and Richard John Neuhaus, eds., *Against the World for the World: The Hartford Appeal and the Future of American Religion* (Nashville, 1976).

[27] Carl F. Henry, 'Where is Modern Theology Going?' *Christianity Today*, XII, No. 11 (1 March 1968), pp. 3–7.

[28] The obvious *lacuna* of a coherent christology in *Honest to God* was recognized by Robinson himself. Its remedy came with *The Human Face of God* (London and Philadelphia, 1973) which was a rather more substantial study. The upshot of it is contained in his essay, 'Our Image of Christ Must Change', *Christian Century*, XC (21 March 1973), pp. 339–342.

[29] Harvey Cox, ' "The Secular City" – Ten Years Later', *Christian Century*, XCII, No. 20 (28 May 1975), p. 546.

[30] Altizer, *Gospel of Christian Atheism,* p. 116.

[31] The symbolism of resurrection always implies return to a higher and antecedent life, so Altizer consistently replaced it by the notion of 'descent into hell'.

[32] Thomas J. J. Altizer, *The Descent into Hell: A Study of the Radical Reversal of the Christian Consciousness* (New York, 1970), pp. 135–169, *Oriental Mysticism and Biblical Eschatology* (Philadelphia, 1961), pp. 113–200.

[33] Cox, *The Secular City,* p. 18.

[34] *Ibid.*, p. 121.

[35] *Ibid.*, p. 128.

[36] *Ibid.*, p. 131.

[37] *Ibid.*, p. 142.

[38] *Ibid.*, p. 165.

[39] Daniel Callahan, ed., *The Secular City Debate* (New York, 1966), p. 214. The areas of interest for Cox's type of 'evangelism' can be discerned from the following essays which he has written: 'Church in East Germany', *Christianity and Crisis*, 23 (22 July 1963), pp. 135–139; 'War on Poverty', *Christianity and Crisis*, 24 (16 November 1964), p. 224; 'Apathy, Abdication, and Acedia', *Renewal*, 5 (January–February 1965), pp. 18–20; 'Mission in a World of Cities', *International Review of Missions*, 55 (July 1966), pp. 273–281; 'Playboy and the Christian', *Theology Today*, 22 (January 1966), pp. 491–499; 'Amnesty for America's Exiles', *Christianity and Crisis*, 28 (25 November 1968), pp. 286–288; 'Penance; from Piety to Politics; Reparations as a Religious and Political Issue', *Renewal*, 7 (June 1967), pp. 18, 19; 'Barbie Doll and the Specter of Cultural Imperialism', *Christianity and Crisis*, 30 (27 April 1970), pp. 81, 82; 'Cultural Captivity of Women', *Christianity and Crisis*, 31 (31 May 1971), pp. 111, 112; 'Viewpoint; who needs Rockefeller?', *Christianity and Crisis*, 34 (11 November 1974), pp. 246, 247.

[40] The most interesting critical essays on Altizer, Cox and Robinson – as judged by the respective editors – are found in Jackson Lee Ice and John J. Carey, eds., *The Death of God Debate* (Philadelphia, 1967); Callahan's *The Secular City Debate*, and David L. Edwards, *The Honest to God Debate* (London and Philadelphia, 1963). See also M. C. McDermott *et al.*, 'Bibliography of the New Theology, II, The New Theologians', *Canadian Journal of Theology*, XIII (April 1967), pp. 134–138.

[41] J. I. Packer, *Keep Yourselves from Idols: A Discussion of the book 'Honest to God'* (London and Grand Rapids, 1964), p. 14.

[42] Cox's theological autobiography is partly contained in his *Seduction of the Spirit: The Use and Misuse of the People's Religion* (New York, 1973). *Cf.* Martin E. Marty, 'Will the Real Harvey Cox Please Stand Up?' *Christian Century*, XCII (28 May 1975), p. 559.

[43] Packer, *Keep Yourself from Idols*, pp. 12, 13.

[44] *Ibid.*, pp. 19, 20.

*We shall find our most fertile field for infiltration of
Marxism within the field of religion, because religious
people are the most gullible and will accept almost
anything if it is couched in religious terminology.*

Lenin

*You were oppressed and fled to the liberated area and
dedicated your life to revolutionary struggle.
I rejoice with you, my brothers.*

**Litany, Bangkok Conference,
World Council of Churches**

*Forward!
Go and teach to use the machine gun;
Resist evil, smite the foolish one on both cheeks;
If you forgive men their faults, you will slow
  down the historical process;
Pray for your enemies only once you have efficiently
  killed them off.
Take your gun and follow me.*

Guillermo Blanco

Chapter Five

Divine politics

Ours is an age of rising expectations, politically, socially, economically; it is also an age of rising frustrations. The Third World, longing to catch up with the West and to enter the promised land of industrialization, now finds itself further from its goal than ever. And within the western democracies themselves, abundance and freedom are not inalienable rights for everyone. The modern world in fact has within it large numbers of people who feel disenchanted, disinherited, outsiders of one sort or another. They see themselves as shut out and deprived, their real potential unrealized because of race, sex, religion or occupation. It is this sense of frustration that is being articulated by a diverse group of theologians who are loosely joined together by a common concern with liberation, the main forum for their work being the World Council of Churches.

Guidelines from the World Council of Churches

The two meetings of the WCC which have proved pivotal for the liberation theologies were the Uppsala Assembly, 1968, and the Bangkok Conference, 1973. At the former, the WCC shifted its concerns from vertical to horizontal issues, from theological questions to involvement in the world, its politics, economic realities and social fabric. At the latter, the WCC gave attention to the theme of 'Salvation Today', clothing the worldly involvement from Uppsala in the language of Christian salvation. There were, however, some interesting steps that led from the assembly to the missionary conference.

In August, 1969, a Consultation was held in Canterbury, England, which addressed the question of salvation. Papers from around the world were presented but the ensuing discussion showed that 'no one account of the meaning of salvation can be universally valid: different aspects are recognized in different historical periods and different cultures'.[1] The feeling that there is not one single gospel or one way of being saved, evident at Canterbury, has been growing. At the same time, the personal element in salvation has been receding. When the theme for the WCC Bangkok meeting was set as 'Salvation Today', it was generally greeted by the non-evangelicals with a tepid response. According to Thomas Wieser, part of the reason for this was that 'the word "salvation" had very little resonance among many Christians'.[2] That this might be due to the absence of a subjective dimension in WCC thought on salvation was later suggested by a participant to the Sixth Ecumenical Seminar, held in Strasbourg in September, 1972. Having listened to a large number of papers on salvation he observed with some concern that in 'almost all of the papers, however, I missed a clear confession of individual, personal salvation'.[3]

When the conference was convened in Bangkok in 1973, the organizers distributed a report designed to provide the participants with an overview of WCC thinking on salvation. The report, entitled *From Mexico City to Bangkok,* suggested that the debate over salvation was focused upon three issues. First, does salvation consist in believing the unchanging truths of the Bible which are the same for all people in every place, or is salvation to be received by entering a worldly process of liberation which may take different forms in different places? Secondly, is salvation essentially concerned with the spiritual and interior life of man or with his political organization and economic relations? Thirdly, does the work of salvation take place more or less within the church, or is God working incognito in men of other religions and in men of no religion? The conferees overwhelmingly chose the second answer in each pair of options.

A majority of those at Bangkok were representatives from the Third World and it was, perhaps, no surprise that the 'western interpretation' of the gospel — meaning largely the first set of options outlined above — should be rejected. The reason given was that Christianity had become enculturated in the West and that the gospel borne by western missionaries to the Third World was simply a means of enslaving the minds of the unevangelized. In the face of the outrage expressed over western enculturation of the gospel, however, it was odd that the conference then went on to provide as controlling frameworks for it African culture, Indian mysticism, and the political ideals of Latin Americans. It would seem that the delegates were not so much complaining about enculturation as they were that they had not had a chance to do this themselves, a deficiency they quickly remedied under the rubrics of 'contextualization' and 'indigenization'.

At Bangkok, the essential definition of salvation which emerged was that of arriving at personal wholeness. To be saved means to realize one's full, human potential. In the Third World, the socio-economic-political order is often an impediment to this and hence this order is sin which needs to be overcome. The conferees therefore declared that 'we see the struggle for economic justice, political freedom and cultural renewal as elements in the total liberation of the world through the mission of God'.[4] Salvation, as a result, is to be worked out in four separate and yet interconnected social dimensions:

1. Salvation works in the struggle for economic justice against the exploitation of people by people.

2. Salvation works in the struggle for human dignity against political oppression of human beings by their fellow men.

3. Salvation works in the struggle for solidarity against the alienation of person from person.

4. Salvation works in the struggle of hope against despair in personal life.[5]

Bangkok in its interpretation of salvation was characterized by strong anti-western feeling. It is interesting to note, for example, that salvation was described as 'the peace of the people in Vietnam, independence in Angola, justice and reconciliation in Northern Ireland and release from the captivity of power in the North Atlantic community'.[6] No indictment, however, was made of Marxist lands, and during the plenary session on China there were those who spoke of it as the world's most Christian country. Salvation in the western democracies was described as 'personal conversion in the release of a submerged society into hope or of new life styles amidst corporate self-interest and lovelessness'.[7] But this typically Marxist analysis of capitalism was not balanced by a typically western critique of the destruction of freedom in Communist countries. Furthermore, the white participants at the conference were put in the dock by the advocates of black power, the disenchanted from the Third World and the Vietnamese sympathizers of the Viet Cong, and held accountable for the various ravages attributed to capitalism throughout the world.[8]

It is not easy, then, to find the specifically theological elements which emerged at Bangkok. Peter Beyerhaus, a delegate at Bangkok and admittedly a severe critic of the WCC, has complained[9] that the organizers were at pains to exclude serious theological work and, instead, staged a series of group encounters with drama, dance and song, added for the benefit of Third World delegates. The closest the conference came to providing a clear theological framework was in the plenary address of the Indian theologian, M. M. Thomas.

Thomas' starting point was an assumption that man's interior life, his spirituality, cannot be isolated from his outward environment. They are interconnected and therefore salvation of the individual soul cannot be considered apart from salvation of the corporate society. For while some societies encourage the development of human potential, others are destructive of it. The reordering of oppressive or debilitating societies, then, constitutes a large part of Christian salvation. It is a salvation, 'not in any pietistic or individualistic isolation, but related to and expressed within the material, social and cultural revolution of our time'.[10] Its goal is to achieve that level of human integration which we see in the Gospel records of Jesus Christ and who today is not a remote, transcendent being abstracted from this world, but an active participant in the movements of liberation.

One of the complaints that Beyerhaus made of Bangkok was that the themes of divine wrath and human guilt, of forgiveness and atonement, were not dealt with at all. The nearest that it came to touching these questions was in the address of Thomas. The 'fall', for example, was given a contemporary interpretation. The world, Thomas declared, goes through socio-political cycles, the high and low points of which are 'creations' and 'falls'. When a country is in a trough, when its system of political power and social order becomes oppressive, then men frantically seek to extricate themselves often without God's help. This, Thomas asserted, is the process of law, sin and death described by Paul in Romans 7. The church's responsibility in this context is to create liberation movements which will free the system's captives. The process of so doing is what constitutes the gospel, and the outcome is the self-conscious recovery of God in the human spirit.

Bangkok, then, is important for its provision of a rough guide as to where WCC thinking is headed on the question of salvation. Yet even the contribution of Thomas leaves unsolved many of the theological questions which naturally arise. In so far as the conference's solution had to be adapted to many different cultural and political contexts, the vagueness of its conception may have been quite deliberate. It will therefore be helpful to move from its statement of general principles to a specific ethnic area, that of South America, to see if the theological details can be elicited with any more clarity.

The task of formulating a theology of liberation in Latin America has been assumed largely by Roman Catholic thinkers, the most prominent of whom are Gustavo Gutiérrez, Juan Segundo and Hugo Assmann.[11] The common concern with developing a theological response to poverty, suffering, deprivation and illiteracy has, however, broken down the traditional barriers between Catholics and Protestants. Joining this enterprise, then, are Protestant theologians such as José Míguez Bonino, Emilio Castro and Rubem Alves. In Europe, a similar outlook has been fashioned by Jürgen Moltmann and Johannes Metz, Protestant and Catholic respectively, and in the United States various ethnotheologies have grown up along roughly the same lines.[12]

The Latin Americans with whom we are principally concerned share two main working assumptions. If these are not always clearly articulated, they are nevertheless always present. The first concerns the notion of *praxis* and the second, an eschatological framework within which their theology is conceived.

Theology by praxis

First, what is meant by *praxis*? On the surface this new concern appears merely as a shift in emphasis from doctrine to practice. It is entirely possible – indeed, in South America it is apparently common – for people to have an obsessive interest in being theologically correct but to have no feeling for the poor and dispossessed, and to assume that existing power structures are what accord most naturally with Christian faith. At the very least, this assumption is being challenged, but in the process a new method of doing theology is emerging. The notion of *praxis* is not, as it may appear, merely the insistence that

123

Christianity be 'practical'; it is, rather, a new way of fashioning a Christian view of things.

Traditionally, theology has begun by formulating 'truths' about God, man and the world. When these 'truths' have been examined, explored and related to one another they are handed on to another set of specialists who work out their practical consequences with respect to ethics, political realities and social issues. It is this process which is under assault by the new thinkers, for they charge that it results in an 'epistemological split' (Gutiérrez) or a 'deep epistemological cleavage' (Míguez Bonino). The cleavage lies between an abstract conception of God on the one side and the hard realities of everyday life on the other. It is a cleavage which is not even bridged by Moltmann[13] and certainly not by the existentialists,[14] who to the Latin thinkers seem to be interested only in personal insights, still less by evangelicals who focus only on interior attitudes.[15] God can no longer be an excuse for not reckoning with the real world.[16]

Praxis as a methodology, therefore, assumes that God is not 'above' the world but is immanently immersed 'in' it. And it assumes that theology is not concerned with abstract theorizing through the means of linguistic and philosophical studies but is, rather, the reflection upon action using the tools of the social and political sciences for its expression. 'Theology', says Gutiérrez, 'does not produce pastoral activity; rather it reflects upon it. Theology must be able to find in pastoral activity the presence of the Spirit inspiring the action of the Christian community.'[17] There are no premises, no antecedent theory beneath the church's action in the world; its action precedes its theology. Theology, in the words of a famous aphorism, is not called upon to describe the world but to change it,[18] and the process of change brings with it the rationale for that change. This, as Assmann notes, represents a 'cultural break from an earlier way of speaking of truth',[19] for 'truth' now becomes synonymous with those actions which change the community for good.

In speaking of this new approach, Segundo makes reference to a 'hermeneutical circle' which, he believes, captures the essence of *praxis*.[20] The circle begins, first, with an experience of reality which leads one to question the prevailing ideologies. This ideological suspicion, secondly, leads one to doubt the prevailing theological assumptions. The questioning of theology, thirdly, leads to exegetical suspicion and this, finally, leads to a new manner of interpreting Scripture.

James Cone's *A Black Theology of Liberation* is praised by Segundo as exemplifying an unbroken circle and hence an approach to theology based on *praxis* which is untarnished. Cone begins with his own experience of being oppressed and disinherited as a black person living in North America. He moves from this experience to identify God with the oppressed community and to arguing that its thrust for liberation in political and economic terms 'is not only consistent with the Gospel but is the Gospel of Jesus Christ'.[21] The fact that his approach is characterized by 'a consciously accepted partiality' does not trouble Cone, for genuine theology – that is, theology relevant to the black community – is accountable only to the black community. The loss of universality is no loss.

Moving into the second stage of the circle, Cone sets out to unmask the nature of oppression, especially as this has repercussions in theology. For thinking about God is one part of a total superstructure throughout all of which the black man is oppressed. The oppression takes place theologically when white theology claims to be colour-blind. In this way sin is discussed in the abstract, as relating to some universal man, and the actual oppression of blacks is not even recognized, still less is it studied.

In the third stage, Cone comes to see exegesis from a different vantage point and with the firm commitment to uncover 'the mechanisms of ideology' and to rout them out of theology. This means that an entirely different set of questions should be posed and the answers which are to be adduced should utilize the sources and norms familiar to the black community rather than white scholars. 'In order to be Christian theology,' Cone affirms, 'White theology must cease being White theology and become Black theology by denying whiteness as a proper form of human existence and affirming blackness as *God's intention for humanity.'*[22] The source of this theology is therefore 'the experience, the history, and the culture of Black people rather than Scripture'.[23] He goes on to affirm that Jesus' teaching and practice can no more be a guide for us today than can Scripture in the making of our decisions.

This does not mean, however, that Cone is unwilling to enter the fourth stage of Segundo's circle, that is, arriving at a new biblical hermeneutic. The resurrection of Christ means that he can be encountered in the world and that he is effecting his liberation through the struggles of oppressed people. Thus the past – Scripture as originally given – must be interpreted in the light of the present – the hopes, desires and plans for liberation of the blacks. Thus divine love can be interpreted as God's solidarity with this community and his wrath as opposition to the oppressive white community.

It is worth noting, in passing, that the completion of this 'hermeneutical circle' which Segundo believes is so exemplary in Cone's case, involves four basic principles. First, Cone assumes the separation of 'Christ' from Jesus; the latter he believes he can disregard provided the former is encountered. Despite his aversion to 'white theology', this apparently is an idea which he has borrowed from it uncritically. Secondly, he has accepted as authoritative, ideas and writings which are not contained within Scripture. The *sola scriptura* principal is jettisoned both for its connections with 'white theology' and its irrelevance to the contemporary struggle of blacks. Thirdly, Cone's complaint about the way in which white theology has become enculturated, becoming the handmaiden of an alien ideology, is apparently only a complaint that blacks have not been as successful at doing this as whites. Cone himself enculturates theology, making it the handmaiden of black liberation ideology. Finally, Cone sees the exegesis of Scripture as being determined by our perceptions of life rather than determining these perceptions. That is what is entailed by *praxis*.

This new approach, Míguez Bonino has argued, is necessary for three reasons. First, metaphysics has collapsed. It is no longer possible to picture the world within a supernatural framework; God is no longer 'above' the world but 'in' it. Secondly, words cannot be separated from a life-context without becoming meaningless. Words have their own coding and decoding devices within the concrete politico-social context in which they arise. Thus a religious word such as *reconciliation* does not carry an abstract meaning that can be transported and applied to every situation in the same way; it is, rather, an antidote to alienation which means different things and requires different action in different situations. Thirdly, the Bible itself always anchors the actions of God within the historical process. It never allows us to take flight into a 'conceptual firmament' where we can spin theologies in the abstract. Consequently Miquez Bonino concludes that there is 'no knowledge except in action itself, in the process of transforming the world through participation in history'.[24]

The identification of religious truth with the transformation of society and the corresponding denial that it can be possessed apart from that transformation, in short, what constitutes *praxis*, is not really new. Its philosophical roots reach into Hegel, Feuerbach and in particular Marx. And it is the Marxian framework which Gutiérrez suggests cannot be superseded for the theologian working in today's world, for it is through Marxism that theology 'has begun to reflect on the meaning of the transformation of this world and the action of man in history'.[25]

A new future for the world

The second working assumption common to these thinkers is that of an eschatology, important aspects of which coincide with the Marxist analysis of the future. As against Bultmann, the theologians of hope like Moltmann − and the liberation and revolutionary theologies which have built on his views − insist that New Testament eschatology must be taken with the utmost seriousness and literalness. Its eschatological elements are essential to Christian faith and cannot be stripped away as if they were only temporary garments. On the other hand, they are hesitant to accept C. H. Dodd's view that some of the eschatological elements have already been realized; more are seen still to be awaiting realization in the future than have been fulfilled in the past. And over against the conservatives, they refuse to allow that any part of the coming *eschaton* has to do with the establishment of a heavenly existence. On the contrary, the New Testament looks forward to a renovation of earthly existence in a completely this-worldly dimension of which Christians should be the contemporary prophets. Both Marx and Moltmann have a 'millennium'; the former's is simply a trifle more secularized than the latter's.[26]

Moltmann, in fact, has been deeply influenced in his theology by Ernst Bloch, the revisionist Marxist philosopher.[27] In particular, he has taken over from Bloch the idea that the world is in a state of flux and is not gelled into rigid forms which can be scientifically described. History, he believes, is open-ended, undecided, unfinished and of an indeterminate character, and man himself has no fixed nature but is pliable, fluid and incomplete. Consequently new possibilities — what he calls the *novum* — are always breaking out. It is this fact alone which encourages us to think that we will have a future qualitatively different from the present, in which will take place what he calls 'the *humanizing* of man, the *socializing* of humanity, *peace* for all creation'.[28] Then will economic inequities be reversed, class alienation overcome, national rivalry eliminated and racial confrontation set aside.

It is evident, however, that this 'millennium' is still far from realization and, in fact, will not come without active involvement by Christians.[29] Moltmann cautiously allows that revolution may be necessary, for the very foundations of our social, political and economic life need to be transformed. Unfortunately, the forces of law and order — judges, policemen, congressmen, members of parliament, armies — are upholders of the *status quo*. As such they are oppressors of millions crushed by a 'system' that does not favour them and is totally uncaring about their needs. Tinkering with it through reform will not achieve the radical transformation that is necessary, only revolution will. This revolution, however, is not simply a destruction of the 'system' but is yoked to the ushering in of a new age. It is this eschatological framework which is the *sine qua non* of liberation theology and it is this which gives it its soul.

Some of the Latin American thinkers can already see an evolution toward the *eschaton* resulting from a driving force within history, pushing toward its future. Both Míguez Bonino and Gutiérrez[30] have discerned in South America three stages on the way to this future. The first was its colonial period, the Spanish dream, which had a religious correspondence in Catholic faith and its expression in processions, pilgrimages and traditional rituals. The second was the neo-colonial period, a time of increasing modernization and industrialization, which found its most appropriate religious expression in Protestantism. It worked, however, at the level of attitudes such as love, truthfulness, integrity, good-will, hard work, and did not seek to change structures. The third stage is now beginning, rising out of the failure of the second.[31] Human life cannot be changed simply at the level of attitudes. People are inextricably a part of the socio-economic-political fabric; without a change in the fabric, those caught within its threads will never enjoy substantial emancipation. That Cuba, situated only seventy miles from the Unites States coast, has succeeded in such a transformation has breathed hope into many a Latin American theologian. It can be done; there are no fixed, immutable laws that stand in the way of its realization.

The common acceptance of these two working assumptions, *praxis* and eschatology, does not mean, however, that liberation theology has reached commonly agreed conclusions wherever it is being developed. In fact, it is still in an experimental stage and its soteriology is only meagerly developed.

Salvation and liberation

The controlling idea of liberation soteriology is undoubtedly 'humanization', although it is not always stated as such, Rubem Alves being the most prominent exception.[32] What redeems this humanism from becoming simply another expression of secularism, it is argued, is that there is an incursion of 'the kingdom of God into the structures of the world'.[33] What is presupposed is that there is alienation between classes, and the recovery of human wholeness, what constitutes salvation, is dependent on the destruction of this alienation.[34] Thus the link between the social analysis of oppression, and the desire to be liberated from it, is God's saving action.

The interest in salvation in its theological as opposed to its sociological dimensions is, as one would expect, difficult to isolate. Gutiérrez, however, begins with an assumption of the unity of God and man and argues that the design of God is to save all people. God's new people 'this time includes all humanity'.[35] There is, he affirms, 'only one human destiny, irreversibly assumed by Christie. . . . His redemptive work embraces all the dimensions of existence and brings them to their fullness'.[36] Gutiérrez, therefore, has no difficulty in affirming that 'the salvific action of God underlies all human existence'.[37] Consequently, he says that the older questions as to how people might be saved, what role the church might play in this process and what happened to those who were not saved, have become irrelevant. God's universal salvific will has been established.

If all men are 'in Christ', 'Christ' is not, however, consciously in all men. The transition in awareness is made as man — be he Christian or non-Christian — opens himself up to God and to others, for God is encountered in others. If this is Gutiérrez's definition of faith, then it follows that conversion is equated with joining the struggle for socio-economic liberation.[38] It is the struggle, divinely initiated, which brings human wholeness.

Adding to this understanding, Segundo contends that the power of God is always humanizing power. Thus in the Gospels the demonic is never presented as an independent source of evil, but rather as 'the prehuman, presocial stage from which Christ and his followers are commissioned to free man'.[39] As such, it is a condition which shows the *incompleteness* of man rather than his inherently evil nature. The Son of God overcomes, not so much personal iniquity, as 'the world', understood as social and political structures. Redemption is collective rather than individual. Segundo stated what is the common consensus when he wrote that 'the later conception of Christianity as a message dealing with individual morality and personal redemption must strike us as a serious distortion'.[40]

From among the other contributors to liberation theology, there is little more that can be added to these basic ideas on salvation. In sum, the objectivity of the atonement is stressed to the point where personal appropriation is eliminated and universalism usually affirmed. The object of Christ's work is not so much personal sin as it is malfunctioning social structures, although there is a tendency among some of these theologians almost to bypass Christ altogether and to concern themselves solely with the incursion of the kingdom of God into this world, seeing its realization among those whom they have identified as oppressed. Many traditional themes are distorted beyond recognition. As Harvey Conn ably notes, 'Salvation is transformed into economic, political liberation, Christology into love of our neighbour, eschatology into politics, church into humanity, sacraments into human solidarity.'[41]

Evaluation

In recent years, theological movements have come and gone with considerable rapidity. Their brief popularity and their noiseless passage into oblivion are alike indicative of the dangerous instability that characterizes Christian thought today. Yet it would be wrong to imagine that these movements had no inner connections or philosophic relations with one another.

Kenneth Hamilton has suggested[42] that Martin Buber in his *The Eclipse of God* articulated an idea which has been widely accepted by the theologies of the 1960s and 1970s. Buber argued that modern man is opposed to the idea of faith, but not to that of religion. Faith assumes the existence of a God who is objectively over against and outside of man, who addresses man in revelation and invites man's response in faith. Modern man has an aversion to that kind of God. He is, however, open to the thought that God is immersing himself in humanity and is coming to ever greater expression within man's self-consciousness. It was this idea that Altizer and the death-of-God theologians articulated and John Robinson seems to have assumed it as well. Its philosophical roots reach into Hegel and its contemporary exponents include the theologians of liberation.

If Moltmann's assumptions are more purely Hegelian, the liberation theologians have entered into the vision of the Young Hegelians who accepted the dialectic of their mentor but focused their attention on the transformation of the world in the present. They asserted that the social fabric always revolves around the distinction between masters and slaves and that all social action must be designed to overcome this distinction. Liberation theology, coming more than a century later, is echoing the Young Hegelians to the letter, the only difference being that whereas they were atheists, these theologians see themselves as Christians.

In terms of theological methodology, therefore, the controlling assumption is the immersion of God in human reality. God is seen as working by, with and under human personality, as pervading it psychologically and coming to realization as people begin to act ethically. The similarities with Freidrich Schleiermacher are inescapable. But if the teaching of Scripture is to be treated with any seriousness at all, it is plain that there is a qualitative, ontological difference between God and man. The God who is emerging within modern self-consciousness, especially within the movements of liberation, is simply not the God and Father of our Lord Jesus Christ. He is a construct of modern philosophical assumptions, the chief of which is man's refusal to believe in a God outside of himself who addresses man through revelation.

The parallels with Schleiermacher's methodology have also produced similarities between liberation theology and the old, discredited social gospel movement.[43] That movement foundered, not so much because of its social concern, as its insipid soteriology. The kingdom of God simply cannot be equated with earthly progress; Jesus himself said that (Jn. 18:36–38; Mt. 26:51–54), and from the time of the medieval Crusades, people have been discovering that utopiae and earthly kingdoms of God are subject to the same type of obsolescence as political kingdoms. Liberation theology will be no exception to a rule already firmly established in history. God is not a political revolutionary ten feet tall.[44]

This assumes, of course, that Moltmann is in error when he argues that history is not bound to immutable ways of working and human nature itself has not gelled. It is on this basis that he looks for a 'millennium' to be achieved, not by the intrusion of Christ into the world, but by man ridding himself of his malfunctioning political and economic systems at some point in the future. It is on this basis that Segundo speaks of man's evolution, Miguez Bonino of a utopia, Alves of messianic humanism and Gutiérrez of freedom. The same kind of talk was heard throughout the Victorian period, captured as it was in the popular slogan 'Every day, in every way, I am getting better and better', and projected philosophically by Marx and ethically by Herbert Spencer in his *The Data of Ethics* (1879). Indeed at the end of the century, in the William Whyte Memorial Lecture, it was seriously argued that man would one day evolve out of war.

Victorian optimism was shattered by the First World War (1914–18) and the theology that had ridden on its crests was attacked as being hopelessly naive, not least by Reinhold Niebuhr in his *Moral Man and Immoral Society*. It is odd, therefore, that given this heritage the liberation theologians are able to function with such short memories.

It is, of course, true that there are some differences to be noted. Liberation theology does not assume, as the old liberal Protestants did, that the ape and tiger in man are simply going to be left behind in the same way that a skin is by an emerging snake. Nothing less than the overthrow of the existing order will achieve this for the liberation thinkers, and for some of them violence is seen as indispensable to the process of evolution. The differences, however, make this movement even less Christian than its liberal forebear. We have it on good authority that those who fight by the sword perish by it, too, and that this is not the way to usher in the kingdom of God. Nor will the justification offered for it suffice. Proponents of revolution argue that established governments constantly commit 'violence' against their subjects by being insensitive to their needs and that violent action taken in the overthrow of the government is, therefore, simply protective concern for the powerless and poor. This is akin to the old suggestion that we should sin in order that grace might abound and that the more we sin, the more it will abound. No end can ever justify such means; that ought to be beyond dispute for any Christian who sees Jesus turning away from the revolutionary zealots and Paul, living under the most oppressive circumstances of Nero's rule, residing his hope, not in revolution, but in the preaching of the kerygmatic gospel.

Furthermore, the type of society for which these theologians hope is not above criticism. Undoubtedly the western democracies are far from perfect and capitalism does produce inequities and injustices. On balance, however, a good case can be made for saying that fewer freedoms are violated under democratic rule than they are under totalitarianisms of the right or left. It is inconceivable that, decadent as western democracy is, twenty million people could be liquidated as happened under Stalin. Likewise, the mass harassments, murder and intimidation of the Chinese cultural revolution or of the Cambodian victors can be seen as desirable only by cold-eyed ideologues or very naive Christians.

Liberation theology, however, is more vulnerable to criticism at the level of its theology than its economics and politics. This is so at three points in particular.

First, Christian faith has become the servant rather than the master of political aspirations. There is no transcendent Word to which everything, including their revolutionary impulses, is subject. 'One is left with the impression', writes René Padilla, 'that the whole question of the kind of action expected of a Christian in a revolutionary situation has been settled *a priori,* and that the role of theology is then merely to provide a façade for this political option.'[45] But it is precisely these *a priori* assumptions that stand in need of critical examination. For despite the Latin Americans' militant resistance to European or 'white' theology, they have naively accepted many modern European ideas. At a social level the theories of Marx and Engels are simply declared to be the best framework around for theological work. At a philosophical level, Hegelian evolutionary theory, made decent by an infusion of biblical language of eschatology,[46] is allowed to guide Christian faith. At a theological level, Barthian universalism, Rahner's notion of the 'supernatural existential' and Pierre Teilhard de Chardin's 'cosmic Christ' are accepted as inviolable *dicta* around which everything else is arranged. The result is that the biblical gospel has been made captive to, rather than being allowed to judge, both culture and ideology. Undoubtedly, as the liberation theologians contend, this has happened in the West, too, but an appropriate remedy is not to outdo the West in its own sinning but to show how the gospel can be expressed through an adopted culture without becoming confused with it.

Secondly, and as a result of this, the doctrine of salvation is seriously perverted. The ultimate distinction between good and evil is blurred, Segundo even arguing that God's redemptive power builds upon the demonic. Therefore, the theme of judgment, so prominent in Scripture, is conspicuous by its absence in liberation theology. It is taken for granted that all men are in Christ. The unexamined rationale for this is an unbalanced application of the classic theory of the atonement which then merges over into the Greek mystical theory in order to accommodate the Hegelian idea of God's immersion in human life. There is, as a result, an unfortunate attempt to 'deprivatize' faith and to rid it of its personal dimensions in favour of overt political action. Any resemblance between this view and what the apostles taught in the early world is more or less coincidental.

Thirdly, the liberation theologians have not distinguished themselves in their exegetical skills despite the fact that some of their works are replete with biblical quotations. Scripture is simply a waxen nose which is bent at will to conform to this or that philosophical propensity. This is seen in innumerable instances but nowhere more plainly than in their handling of the exodus narrative.

This event, Alves declares, is the central principle of organization of the whole biblical revelation. Gutiérrez sees it as a paradigm of what God is doing throughout the world. What the exodus reveals is how God, on behalf of his covenant people, overthrew a political order and saved them in terms that are starkly physical. Gutiérrez, of course, has no place for the idea of a covenant people for he sees salvation as now embracing the whole of humanity, but he does believe that the exodus gives us the key to how God saves today. What neither Gutiérrez nor Alves has examined, however, is how Scripture itself interprets the exodus. Instead, this event is simply wrenched from its over-all biblical context and made to do service in the cause of contemporary political liberation.

Francis Foulkes,[47] for example, has shown how in Old Testament prophetic literature the first exodus was slowly reinterpreted as the hope began to grow that God would re-enact this great event at some point in the future. The same elements of deliverance from captivity, divine succour in the wilderness, water from the rock, protection from the sun and the divine presence before the people all reappear (Is. 40:3; 43:19ff.; 49:10; 51:10ff.; 52:3–12). There is, however, a difference, for while some of the physical elements are retained in this hope, others are already falling away. The exodus, like so many of the other elements of Old Testament salvation, is becoming internalized and spiritualized. 'Egypt' in Hosea's thought is synonymous with and a symbol of the sinfulness of man's nature (7:16; 8:13; 9:3; 11:5) and the elements of salvation which follow, if historical, are also in places adapted to this process. Commenting on this, R. E. Nixon notes that 'this is developed further in the idea of the second "Exodus" in Jeremiah 16:14ff.; 23:7ff. The process has its full flower in the prophecies connected with the Exile, to be found in Ezekiel and Isaiah 40–55.'[48] The prophecy in Ezekiel 20 sees Israel as having been redeemed from herself as much as from the Egyptians and the Isaianic prophecies pick up the spiritual exodus in terms of a new Messianic Moses.

The New Testament reasserts this theme, in terms not of hope but of realization. The aged Simeon recalls the passage from Isaiah about the second exodus and applies it to Christ, and at point after point thereafter the exodus motif is repeated. The parallels between Jesus on the one hand and Moses and Joshua on the other are hinted at in the Gospels and declared in the epistles. In John 6, there is an explicit linking of New Testament salvation to the Old Testament manna. Paul specifically refers to Christ as our 'paschal lamb' (1 Cor. 5:7ff.) and to Christians as the New Israel who are redeemed through the new Passover. In all of this, he sees salvation coming, not through the overthrow of the political order, but by the faith acceptance of the

135

preached *kerygma* concerning the substitionary death of Christ in atonement and his vindication by the Spirit in resurrection. Liberation theology has to earn credibility by careful biblical exegesis along these lines; it cannot assume that it is credible as Christian theology simply on the grounds that it is the product of the Third World.

In spite of these deficiencies, liberation theology can have a positive influence in two areas if the western academic community will allow it to. First, it has called attention to how easily biblical truth becomes enculturated. Unfortunately, the proponents of liberation have gone on to spoil everything by enculturating the gospel themselves in a far-reaching manner. If the West is to learn anything from this, it will be by heeding what liberation theologians say and not by observing what they do. Secondly, liberation theology has rightly excoriated western, academic thought for its frequent preoccupation with worthless speculative ventures. Not only have theologians failed dismally in communicating with ordinary people, but they have often failed to see that Christians should be actively engaged in changing the world for good rather than merely talking about it or describing it abstractly. Yet having said that, it has to be added that social action is at most the corollary to, or the context for, the kerygmatic gospel, and is never its substance. In the final analysis, a person is saved, not by having his bank balance augmented or by receiving medical attention, but by believing that in the crucified Christ his sins were pardoned and his guilt was covered.

Notes

[1] 'Salvation Today; Issues for Further Study', *Study Encounter*, 4 (1969), p. 209.

[2] Thomas Wieser, 'Giving Account of Salvation Today', *Study Encounter*, XI, No. 1 (1975), p. 1.

[3] Heinrich Voges, 'Jesus – Solution or Salvation?' *Lutheran World*, XX, No. 3 (1973), pp. 261, 262.

[4] Gerald H. Anderson and Thomas F. Stransky, *Mission Trends*, II, *Evangelization* (Grand Rapids, 1975), p. 236. The full documents and related essays are also published in *International Review of Mission*, 62, No. 246 (April 1973). pp. 136–230.

[5] *Ibid.*, p. 237.

[6] *Ibid.*, p. 238.

[7] *Ibid.*

[8] Peter Beyerhaus, *Bangkok 73: The Beginning or End of World Mission?* (Grand Rapids, 1973), pp. 45–52.

[9] Peter Beyerhaus, 'Theology of Salvation in Bangkok', *Christianity Today*, 17, No. 13 (30 March 1973), pp. 11–17.

[10] M. M. Thomas, 'The Meaning of Salvation Today', *International Review of Missions*, LXII, No. 246 (April 1973), p. 162. Thomas' position is explained more fully in his study *Salvation and Humanization* (Madras, 1971), but see also his 'Salvation and Humanization: A Crucial Issue in the Theology of Mission in India', *International Review of Missions*, 60 (January 1971), pp. 28–38. For Thomas, it is clear, the fundamental differences are not those that divide, say, Buddhists and Hindus from Christians, but those that divide people who are 'open' and full of self-awareness from those who are not. Elsewhere he says that this view really derives from Barthian dialectical theology, 'which emphasises the transcendence of the Word and Deed of God in Jesus Christ over all religions and quasi-religions of mankind'. This, he goes on, 'has provided the basis for a radical relativisation of all religions including Christianity and also of Atheism; and its understanding of Jesus Christ as the humanism of God rejecting and electing all mankind in Jesus Christ points to a transcendent power which can renew them all'. M. M. Thomas, *Man and the Universe of Faiths* (Madras, 1975), p. 147. This and similar views were rejected by the signers of the Frankfurt Declaration, 1970, as being derogatory to the Christian gospel. See Peter Beyerhaus, *Missions: Which Way? Humanization or Redemption* (Grand Rapids, 1971). The history of the Frankfurt Declaration is covered in his *Shaken Foundations. Theological Foundation for Mission* (Grand Rapids, 1972), pp. 63–75.

[11] A bibliography of over 700 entries of mainly primary sources covering the decade 1964–74 is published by C. Peter Wagner, ed., *A Catalog of the C. Peter Wagner Collection of Materials on Latin American Theology of Liberation* (Pasadena, 1974); on the main figures, see also James F. Conway, *Marx and Jesus: Liberation Theology in Latin America* (New York, 1973), pp. 210–221.

[12] Omitted from discussion are the American feminists whose views can be encountered, for example, in Letty M. Russell, *Human Liberation in a Feminist Perspective – A Theology* (Philadelphia, 1974) and Rosemary Reuther's latest volumes *New Woman, New Earth* (New York, 1975) and *From Machismo to Mutuality* (New York, 1975), partly summarized in her 'Sexism and the Theology of Liberation; Fall and Salvation as seen from the Experience of Women', *Christian Century*, 90 (12 December 1973), pp. 124–129. In addition, there are various ethnotheologies which have had to be omitted, as represented by: James H. Cone's studies, *Black Theology and Black Power* (New York, 1969) and *A Black Theology of Liberation* (Philadelphia, 1970), Vine Delovia, *God is Red* (New York, 1973), and Armando B. Rendon, *Chicano Manifesto* (New York, 1971). See Michael Berenbaum, 'Women, Blacks, and Jews: Theologians of Survival', *Religion in Life*, 45, No. 1 (Spring 1976), pp. 106–118.

[13] Jürgen Moltmann, 'On Latin American Liberation Theology: An Open Letter to José Míguez Bonino', *Christianity and Crisis*, XXXVI, No. 5 (29 March 1976), pp. 57–63.

[14] The reaction against existential theology began with the 'theology of hope' and the 'political theology'. Having declared that the existentialist hermeneutic 'remains imprisoned within the circle of a private I-and-thou relationship', Metz went on to declare that the *reversal of this privatizing tendency is the primary critical task of political theology*'. Johannes Metz, 'The Church's Social Function in the Light of a "Political Theology"', *Concilium:* Vol. 36, *Faith and the World of Politics* (New York, 1968), pp. 3–5.

[15] José Míguez Bonino, *Doing Theology in a Revolutionary Situation* (Philadelphia, 1975), pp. 11–15.

[16] The disenchantment among liberation theologians is felt both toward the church in Latin America which, it is charged, has sanctioned the political *status quo* thereby oppressing the poor, and the church in the western democracies which has sanctioned economic imperialism. All of the plans for developing the Third World have failed and the cause of the failure, it is believed, is the inherent economic need of the developed nations to keep the underdeveloped nations underdeveloped. See Míguez Bonino, *Doing Theology in a Revolutionary Situation*, pp. 16–18; Juan Segundo, 'Wealth and Poverty as Obstacles to Development', *Human Rights and the Liberation of Man in the Americas*, ed. Luis M. Colonnese (Notre Dame, 1970), pp. 23–31; *cf.*

Samuel Escobar's different perspective in his essay 'The Social Impact of the Gospel', *Is Revolution Change?* ed. Brian Griffiths (London, 1972: Downers Grove, 1973), pp. 84–105.

[17] Gustavo Gutiérrez, *A Theology of Liberation: History, Politics and Salvation*, trans. and ed. Caridad Inda and John Eagleson (New York, 1973: London, 1974), p. 11.

[18] The source of this well-known dictum is, of course, Marx, but it has captured the essence of liberation thought, as has a friend of Hugo Assmann in these lines: 'When you succeed in changing/all your abstract nouns/for a few concrete ones/whose meaning can be felt,/perhaps it will make sense again/for you to talk to us of Christ and God./When it is seen to be true,/in a way that can be genuinely proclaimed,/that Justice has 'pitched its tent in our midst',/and that Love has 'dwelt amongst us',/then perhaps what your Bible calls/the 'name of God'/can make itself known." Hugo Assmann, *Theology for a Nomad Church*, trans. Paul Burns (New York, 1976), p. 25.

[19] *Ibid.*, p. 19.

[20] Juan Luis Segundo, *Liberation of Theology*, trans. John Drury (New York, 1975), pp. 7–38.

[21] Cone, *A Black Theology of Liberation*, as quoted in Segundo, *Liberation of Theology*, p. 26.

[22] Cone, *A Black Theology of Liberation*, pp. 32, 33 as quoted in Segundo, *Liberation of Theology*, pp. 29, 30.

[23] *Ibid.*, p. 30.

[24] Míguez Bonino, *Doing Theology in a Revolutionary Situation*, p. 98.

[25] Gutiérrez, p. 9. See Edgar C. Bundy, ed., *The Marxist-Revolutionary Invasion of the Latin American Churches* (Wheaton, 1972). The tone of Bundy's volume is somewhat belligerent but it contains solid documentation.

[26] The Latin American theologians have been somewhat critical of Moltmann but there can be little doubt that his theology of hope has been deeply influential. Thus Gutiérrez writes that 'the Bible presents eschatology as the driving force of salvific history radically oriented toward the future. Eschatology is thus not just one more element of Christianity, but the very key to understanding the Christian faith' (p. 162). *Cf.* Rubem Alves, *A Theology of Human Hope* (Washington, 1969), pp. 85–105.

[27] See Bernard R. Ramm, 'Ethics in the Theology of Hope', *Toward a Theology for the Future*, ed. Clark Pinnock and David F. Wells (Carol Stream, 1971), pp. 189–216.

[28] Jürgen Moltmann, *The Theology of Hope: On the Ground and Implications of a Christian Eschatology* (London and New York, 1967), p. 329.

[29] Jürgen Moltmann, *Religion, Revolution and the Future* (New York, 1969). See also his essays 'Liberation in the Light of Hope', *Ecumenical Review*, 26 (July 1974), pp. 413–429; 'Theological Basis of Human Rights and of the Liberation of Man', *Reformed World*, 31 (December 1971), pp. 348–357. The issue of whether violence is a viable option for a Christian has polarized the Latin Americans. See, for example, José Míguez Bonino, 'Violence and Liberation', *Christianity and Crisis*, 32 (10 July 1972), pp. 169–172; 'Violence; a Theological Reflection', *Ecumenical Review*, 25 (October 1973), pp. 68–74; Rubem Alves, *A Theology of Human Hope*, p. 155. *Cf.* the general but incisive study on the subject by Jacques Ellul, *Violence: Reflections from a Christian Perspective* (New York, 1969: London, 1970).

[30] Gutiérrez, p. 215; Míguez Bonino, *Doing Theology in a Revolutionary Situation*, pp. 2–20.

[31] The evolution of Latin America has left some doubt as to whether Protestantism can have a future on that continent, and what its contribution might be. See especially Juan Segundo, 'Possible Contribution of Protestant Theology to Latin American Christianity in the Future', *Lutheran Quarterly*, 22 (February 1970), pp. 60–68; Rubem Alves, 'Is There a Future for Protestantism in Latin America?' *Lutheran Quarterly*, 22 (February 1970), pp. 49–59.

[32] Alves, *A Theology of Human Hope*, pp. 85–100.

[33] Gang Beinert, *The Digest*, 24, No. 1 (Spring 1976), p. 25.

[34] The assumption which is made in this political salvation is that the oppressed proletariat in

Marxist philosophy corresponds to the 'poor' in biblical language. Thus Rubem Alves can speak of God's creation of a counter-culture among the poor and the formation of this new consciousness, which is political in nature, as the creation of the New Man. (See Rubem Alves, *Tomorrow's Child: Imagination, Creativity and the Rebirth of Culture* [London and New York, 1972], p. 202. *Cf.* Míguez Bonino, *Doing Theology in a Revolutionary Situation*, pp. 106–111.) Whether these two concepts can be equated so easily is a debatable question.

[35] Gutiérrez, p. 158.

[36] *Ibid.*, p. 153.

[37] *Ibid.*

[38] José Míguez Bonino, 'Theology and Liberation', *International Review of Missions*, 61 (January–October 1972), pp. 70–72.

[39] Juan Luis Segundo, *Evolution and Guilt*, trans. John Drury (New York, 1974), p. 72.

[40] *Ibid.*, p. 52.

[41] Harvey M. Conn, 'The Mission of the Church', *Evangelicals and Liberation*, ed. Carl E. Armerding (Nutley, NJ, 1977), p. 82.

[42] Kenneth Hamilton, 'Liberation Theology: An Overview', *Evangelicals and Liberation*, pp. 1–9.

[43] See Robert T. Handy, ed., *The Social Gospel in America* (New York, 1966). There are close parallels, too, with the Christian Social movement associated with F. D. Maurice. See W. Merlin Davies, *An Introduction to F. D. Maurice's Theology* (London, 1964), and Alec R. Vidler, *F. D. Maurice and Company: Nineteenth Century Studies* (London, 1966).

[44] Peter Wagner has rightly warned of the danger of equating any one political option with the imperishable gospel. A passion for social action, if it takes this route, can end up inverting biblical priorities and denying the gospel to the vast proportion of people who do not share the adopted political outlook. C. Peter Wagner, *Latin American Theology: Radical or Evangelical?* (Grand Rapids, 1970), p. 32. On the general subject see Alan Richardson, *The Political Christ* (London, 1973).

[45] René Padilla, 'The Theology of Liberation', *Christianity Today*, 18, No. 3 (9 November 1973), p. 69.

[46] The concept of hope in the New Testament is briefly examined by C. F. D. Moule in his *The Meaning of Hope* (Philadelphia, 1963). His conclusion, based on careful exegesis, is that in the main it pertains to the interior relationship with Christ and he finds no political utopia in its teaching.

[47] Foulkes, pp. 21, 22.

[48] R. E. Nixon, *The Exodus in the New Testament* (London, 1963), p. 9.

His wallet lay before him in his cap
Brimful of pardons from the very seat
In Rome. . . .
He would get more money in a single day
Than in two months would come the parson's way.

Geoffrey Chaucer

She changes her methods, but not her spirit.

Lorraine Boettner

Christ summons the Church, as she goes her pilgrim
way, to that continual reformation of which she
always has need, insofar as she is an institution of
men here on earth.

Second Vatican Council

There are many kinds of disillusionment in the post-
conciliar Church. . . .

James Hitchcock

Chapter Six

Roman Catholic theology

Even to the casual observer it is plain that Roman Catholicism is in a period of transition. Meat on Fridays, nuns in contemporary dress, priests in wedlock, guitars in the Mass and the laity in some confusion all witness to this fact. Indeed, it would not be going too far to say that Catholics are being caught up in a new search for religious self-identity. The outward changes are really indicative of a deeper mutation in the underlying *mentalité* itself, and this has a direct bearing on the way that salvation is being conceived.

The traditional teaching on salvation, then, first needs to be recalled before the changes of more recent days can be described and analysed. If we are still allowed to use the Council of Trent as a point of departure, these ideas might be sketched accordingly. When man was first created, God set before him the goal to which he was to attain. This was to see God in his unveiled glory (the beatific vision). Man was also given the means of reaching this end. He was given the bent and desire to do good (created grace[1]) and he was instructed that co-operation with this inward orientation would lead him to his destination. When the fall occurred, man's nature was fractured and its perversion (original sin) was passed on from generation to generation. Certainly this perversion brought with it twisted and illicit desires; certainly the desires brought forth acts which were blameworthy. But the intrusion of sin did not destroy the capacity to do good; it merely rendered the potential for good inert.

The life and death of the incarnate Son of God achieved two main goals. First, it secured forgiveness for all, but this is made effective only in those who, through baptism, have been joined to his body, the Roman Catholic Church. Baptism provides the grace (known as sanctifying grace) by which a person is regenerate. So, secondly, such a person can once again be related to God, the basis of it being what Christ did in his death and what the sinner does in his life to live out

141

the virtues of faith, hope and love. Justification, however, is not a declaratory act but a life-process. A person is not justified by exercising saving faith in the finished work of Christ; he might *become* justified through a life-time of obedience to Church teaching and nourishment from the Church's sacraments. What is left undone in this system of achieving personal rectitude can be completed in purgatory. But this does mean that outside of a personal revelation from God, no-one can know for certain whether or not he is saved, since no-one knows for certain whether or not his or her virtue is complete.[2]

Some of these ideas, given here in a rudimentary form to be sure, have become the object in recent times of intense re-examination. This new work has generally fallen into three main categories: first, that which has explored the meaning of grace; second, that which has examined the role of Church in salvation; third, that which has reworked the nature of faith and the doctrine of justification.

New views of grace

In its spirit and temper, recent Catholic theology has departed considerably from its older, scholastic forebear. It hardly ever begins with unabashed metaphysical commitments, philosophical *a priori* and antecedent considerations as did the older orthodoxy. Instead of looking at theology from God's point of view, the new theology looks at it from man's. Indeed, it looks at it through the filter of man's own experience[3] so the results are more blurred, tentative and psychologically tinted than ever before. As a result, the old opposition to culture, in particular to secular culture, has largely disappeared. The doctrine of grace, therefore, can be comfortably analysed, not as something that is alien to human life and other-worldly, but as a common ingredient in human experience.[4] It might be objected, of course, that this will entail putting new content into old form.[5] And so it might. But proponents of the new theology argue that their intent is merely that of giving fresh statement to the old doctrine without actually violating it. Their design is to develop Catholic doctrine but never to change it.[6]

The core idea in Catholic soteriology is found in its distinction between nature[7] and grace and it is not surprising that theologians have been giving this concept considerable attention.[8] Nature has customarily been defined as having two parts. First, it has a passive capacity for God (*potentia obedientialis*); in more common language, we might say that in each man there is a God-shaped blank which can be filled by God alone. Secondly, nature has a desire for grace (*desiderium naturale*). This desire is like an instinct or an ache; it is to the spirit what the pangs of hunger are to the stomach. The fact that man has both the capacity and appetite for God does not mean that God is *obliged* to meet man's need. Indeed, the distinction between nature and grace was first set up to show that God was not so obliged. Grace, which in Catholic theology is defined more as divine life than as divine forgiveness, is quite distinct from nature because God is quite distinct from man. And if man's inward emptiness and need for God are to be satisfied it will only be because God in his compassion brings himself to meet man's need and never because he was under compulsion to do so.[9]

The contemporary exploration of grace is associated most frequently with the name of Karl Rahner. Undoubtedly his work rests on the conclusions of others such as J. Maréchal, M. De La Taille, Henri de Lubac and even Maurice Blondel, the largely unknown French philosopher who worked on the fringes of modernism at the turn of the century. What Rahner has done has, of course, also been extended and developed by others. Yet there can be little question about his seminal contribution especially as this has its focus in his notion of the 'supernatural existential'.[10]

Rahner begins by distinguishing between the supernatural existential and the sanctifying grace of baptism. In other words, his analysis begins with man as *man*, before he ever comes within the structure of the Church and is affected by its sacraments. His argument is that in his 'raw' nature, man is not inert and cut off from the realm of the divine. The older orthodoxy said that man had the equipment to hear God but that this equipment had to be pushed into operation by God; Rahner argues that the equipment is present and is already working through God's initiative in all men. Man not only has an ear but is *actively* listening. So while it is proper to distinguish between nature and grace in order to protect the idea that it is God who takes the initiative in saving man, the fact of the matter is that nature has never existed in separation from grace. Grace infuses nature and, in a sense, is a part of our humanity. Being human means not only having an

143

inner vacuum that only God can fill but also having an active predisposition for and sense of God.

This supernatural existential gives to all men a context, a dimension, an atmosphere in which they can function and from which they can never escape. It is an ethos which is neither natural nor material. It is part of our common, human experience even if it is also supernatural. It is distinguishable from nature and yet it always determines man's choices from within; it never impinges on his life as an alien force from without but is experienced as a part of man's own self. Man knows the supernatural, not as an effect does its cause, but as a husband does his wife through union.[12] This structure is permanent.

The supernatural existential, then is the *sine qua non* of salvation. Rahner and many other contemporary Catholics have been greatly troubled as to how a reconciliation can be effected between God's apparent universal design in salvation and the particularism of the means used to reach this end, the Roman Catholic Church. For Roman Catholics continue to decline in proportion to the rest of mankind and especially that part of it which is unchurched and untaught in Christian terms. Solutions to the problem have been advanced in the past, but many of their proponents simply have not grasped the enormity of the problem. It is a problem with two aspects. First, with what endowments does God have to equip men in order that all might have the possibility of being saved? Secondly, what relationship do they need to sustain to the visible Church in order to be saved? The supernatural existential is concerned primarily with the first of these questions, namely, the subjective condition. With this notion of the supernatural existential, Rahner is developing along metaphysical lines what is rather more common in ethical discussions. In ethics, the question often discussed is Kant's: 'Does I ought mean I can?' Transposing this, does the obligation on all men to know God and love him with all of their being mean that they have the inherent capacity to do so? Rahner believes, with a few qualifications, that it does. For to say that all are destined for the beatific vision and that all should be preparing for this without assuming that God provides the means to this end is to make a mockery, he believes, of both language and morality.

What God gives to each person in order that he might reach this end is not simply intermittent impulses of divine life, or occasional glimpses of some kind of mystery in the world, but a steady and steadying determination from within that impells man towards God. It is an urging which persists regardless of whether man recognizes its presence, interprets it aright or responds to it as God designed. The end that all men might see God is therefore linked up to the means by which they can do this. The means itself derives from the life and death of Christ. Christ's work encompasses all men and affects all men at this level. Man's self-experience would be different had God never been enfleshed at Bethlehem and crucified at Calvary. In general, if not in particular, all men are in Christ.

If the saving will of God embraces all men and there exists the possibility that all might be saved, then what content needs to be put into the act of belief? If all can be saved what do they need to believe to be saved and from where do they derive it? Traditionally, of course, there were many truths which were necessary for salvation which were not given by the light of natural reason and of which the Church was the custodian and dispenser. To receive these truths one had to be received within the Church but this simply poses in its starkest form the question as to how God can have universal saving intentions if the only means he uses to reach this end are so exclusive.

Even before the Second Vatical Council, Max Seckler[13] proposed a solution which, if it appeared a trifle *avant-garde,* contained ideas which have subsequently been widely embraced. He argued that sufficient supernatural revelation is given within man for salvation. It is located in an 'instinct' which is an essential part of nature. This intuitive sense is related to verbalized revelation not merely as a part is to the whole play but also as the understudy is to the main actor. Verbalized revelation clarifies and enlarges what is already in man, rather than superseding and replacing it.

It is clear that Seckler's notion or one very like it underlies the Council's discussion of non-Christian religions.[14] The Council asserted that all men have a common origin, comprise a single community and are destined to the same end.[15] As parts of the whole, different religions reflect on the mystery of life in different ways; God's grace is, in varying proportions, found in them, too. For this reason, Catholics were enjoined to 'acknowledge, preserve and promote the spiritual and moral goods found among these men'.[16] They are not to be condemned, but seen, rather, as being implicitly Christian even if their religious life is flawed. The Council was quite firm in its view that the faith-experience of an adherent of a non-Christian religion is salvific if it is based on the desire to please God by good works as these are prompted through the conscience.[17] 'What we have called the "unbeliever" or "non-Christian",' comments Thomas Stransky, 'is saved insofar as he is a believer by a salvific faith that is already, in some way, both Christian and ecclesial.'[18]

Perhaps the most interesting application that Rahner himself makes of the supernatural existential is in his idea of the 'anonymous Christian'.[19] There are evidently many people in the world who sustain a positive relation to the redemptive work of Christ but who stand outside of the visible structure of the Roman Church. To say that they are all lost would deny what Christ has done for them and in them, and yet to admit that they can be fully saved without the aid of the Church would be to undercut what is the essence of Catholicism, its doctrine of the Church. Rahner therefore distinguishes between the broader 'people of God' and that part of it contained within the Roman Church.

The nature-grace distinction is, of course, rather foreign to Protestant discourse and the subtleties of the discussion are sometimes hard to comprehend. To change the key, what it amounts to is this. Unregenerate man is not excluded from divine fellowship. The basis of this fellowship is not merely a dim knowledge about God's existence (what in Protestant discourse is called natural revelation) but also an experience of that kind of grace which saves. This experience is the common property of all, of atheists as well as the self-consciously religious. The response to this grace varies as does the truthfulness of a person's understanding of it, yet it can no more be excluded from human life than can soil from a garden. It is the atmosphere which we all breathe, consciously or unconsciously. For a Catholic this poses an acute problem in another area, for it seems to suggest that the Church is now no longer necessary for salvation.

The Church and salvation

What is the role of the church in bringing salvation to people? The answer, in terms of traditional theology, has always been direct and simple. Outside of the Church there has been no salvation. This, as J. J. King has argued, has implied two things. First, union with the Church in some form precedes salvation, for the Church is the means without which salvation cannot be obtained. Secondly, if actual union with the Church was not possible, God would recognize in its stead the desire for it (*votum ecclesiae*). Thus a visible union was not always necessary but complete separation was never acceptable.[20]

In 1953, a Boston priest, Father Leonard Feeney, had to be excommunicated for his insistence on a strict interpretation of the *extra ecclesiam nulla salus* formula. The precise reason for his excommunication has been widely discussed, but the papal letter to Cardinal Cushing bearing on this case (*Suprema haec sacra*[21]) has been used to give a different interpretation to the old formula.

Yves Congar, for example, in his book *The Wide World My Parish: Salvation and Its Problems*, argues that the formula has always been understood negatively, as condemning those not within the visible structure of the Church. Now, he suggests, it might be understood more positively as declaring that it is through the Roman Catholic Church that God intends to extend his saving purposes to the whole world. It is a shift away from the subjects of salvation − who can and cannot be saved − to the means of salvation, the Church. As a counterweight to the argument that specific knowledge derived from the Church and its revelation is necessary for the completion of faith, he sets the biblical texts which indicate that within man there is a law according to which he will be judged. It is in this openness to God that the 'intention of faith' lies.[22]

Congar's argument therefore coalesces with Rahner's in seeing that membership in the Church of Rome is not simply a matter either of being in or out of the Church. There are *degrees* of membership.[23] While it is true that the greater part of mankind is not visibly a part of the Church, there is a different and invisible type of membership which, if not juridical, is nevertheless still real. For where salvation is, there also is the Church even if it has escaped its legal and visible structures. The end result, therefore, is to invert the old formula.

Salvation was once dependent on the Church; the Church now accompanies salvation. The Church extends as far as the number of saved do, even to those who say explicitly that they are not Roman Catholics.

The Second Vatican Council treated this issue with considerable delicacy. While it affirmed the old formula that outside the Church there is no salvation and, in fact, quoted directly from *Suprema haec sacra*,[24] it also allowed that there are degrees of membership in the Church. The second chapter of the Constitution on the Church, *Lumen gentium*, is entitled 'The People of God'. This 'people' is larger in number than these who belong to the visible, hierarchial Church described in the constitution's third chapter. In subtly devised language, it went on to articulate these differing degrees of membership, asserting that some of the elements of authentic membership are found in communions other than the Roman. Thus while Catholics were said to be 'incorporated' and their incorporation to be 'full', non-Catholic Christians were said merely to be 'linked'. If their relation is not as satisfactory as that of Catholics, it needs to be noted that the Council allowed (for the first time) that they had churches and, further, they are not ultimately separated from God. Finally, even non-Christians could be described as being 'related'.[25] Karl Rahner is among those who believe that the qualities of relationship implied here mean that the term 'People of God' can be extended to all of humanity.[26]

New work on justification

The third general area on which some of the new theological work has been focused is that of faith and justification. The definitive statement of traditional teaching on both themes is obviously found in the decrees of the Council of Trent. This council met after the Reformation in order to set the Catholic Church in order and to refute the heretics. In recent years, however, Catholic scholarship has undertaken fresh analysis of Trent. The progression of volumes on Luther from Catholic authors has also become increasingly benign toward him.[27] With respect to both the Council and Luther, it has become commonplace to draw a distinction between the truth expressed and the mode of its expression. In the case of the Council, it is frequently argued that its defensive posture *vis-à-vis* the Protestant renegades produced teaching which was true in its historic context but which needs now to be modified. Hans Küng, of course, has gone beyond this to assert that infallibility can never be found, regardless of whether one is looking at Scripture, the Church, the Pope or even councils. This brash assault on his own Church created no small furore and precipitated a spectacular theological clash with Rahner but is generally seen to be too *avant-garde* for comfort.[28] Hubert Jedin in his definitive study on the council,[29] however, offers a *via media* between virtually discarding Tridentine teaching on the grounds of its human relativity, and refusing to consider, on the grounds of its divine character, any historic conditioning in its statements. If, indeed, such conditioning is present, the conciliar decree on justification may be re-examined with a view to its ultimate reformulation. With respect to Luther, there is increasing recognition by Catholic scholars that the moribund condition of the Church which the German reformer assailed was no mere figment of his imagination. Far from being the lamentable syphilitic, the demented sot whose own moral decay produced his easy doctrine of grace, as Denifle and Grisar claimed, contemporary scholars such as Joseph Lortz and Küng more frequently see him as being among the Church's most pious and brilliant theologians whose chief error was not his doctrine of justification by faith alone but his impatience in refusing to stay within the Church and submit to it. The existence of these two new lines of historical interpretation seem to have paved the way for a different understanding of justification from that usually associated with the Tridentine decrees.

Prior to the Council, the most brilliant and startling reworking of the doctrine was produced by Küng who also managed to incorporate most of this new thinking into his study.[30] The appearance of his book, which contained an analysis of Barth's doctrine of justification and a demonstration of its compatibility with Catholic views, was made all the more remarkable by the accompanying prefatory letter from Barth. In this he 'gladly, gratefully, and publicly' testified that Küng's exposition of his own thought was accurate, balanced and precise. He naturally expressed his 'considerable amazement' at Küng's thesis, and confessed his puzzlement at how such themes as God's free grace, justification by faith alone, and the substitutionary death of Christ had lain concealed in the Tridentine decrees and canons unnoticed for so long.

149

Küng in his positive exposition saw justification as having an objective and subjective aspect. Barth, he suggested, as a contemporary exponent of Reformation views, had focused on the former in which man is passive and the interest is on what God has done for man through Christ. Trent concerned itself with the latter in which man is active, appropriating the grace by which Christ lives in men. The teaching of the council on this aspect arose in reaction to the Lutheran emphasis, but this did not mean that the objective side was denied. Indeed, the discussion on justification – what in historic Protestantism is meant by sanctification – was prefaced, Küng argued, by a section on redemption which is the Catholic counterpart to (objective) justification for a Protestant. The two aspects, passive and active, objective and subjective, are complementary not contradictory and, said Küng, the Council of Trent affirmed them both.

Küng defined justification as 'the declaration of justice by God who at the cross and in the resurrection of Jesus Christ declares all sinners free and just', but the sinners must submit 'in faith to God's verdict' for it to have subjective consequences.[31] He acknowledged that faith contains the element of trust (*fiducia*) along with that of credence (*fides*) and denied that this can be regarded as a 'work'. God and man are not, he said, pulling on the same rope. He refuted synergism and affirmed grace as God's personal favour extended to all through Christ but received only in faith. Thus he was able to declare the unabridged universality of grace (for *all* men are justified in Christ) its complete gratuity (for it is never earned) and its enduring primacy (for no good work arises without it).

Given Barth's endorsement of the volume and the loud ecumenical acclaim which followed its appearance, it may appear somewhat churlish either to question the validity of Küng's thesis or to question whether he did, through Barth, come to terms with the Protestant Reformers. Yet there are grounds for doubt on both scores. Barth himself was apparently dubious on the first point and asked Küng humorously whether he had seen all of these truths in the Tridentine decrees before or after reading the *Church Dogmatics!*

On the second point, it needs to be observed that nothing which Küng said in his book was really incompatible with the nature-supernature correlation which Rahner and others had been refining,[32] and it was with this, rather than papal authority or tradition, that the

Reformation was centrally concerned. The original intention of the distinction between nature and grace had been to outlaw Pelagianism. It was Luther's contention, however, that the distinction was neither clear nor sharp enough, with the result that Pelagianism had in fact invaded the Church's teaching. The infusion of grace in nature resulted in the incorporation of works into the basis of acceptance before God.

The seeds of this outlook, however, are not particularly evident in Küng's study on justification, but they have become more plain in his massive *summa* entitled *On Being a Christian* and published a decade later. It is true that his new book is more of an apologetic for Christian faith than it is a work of technical theology. Küng's capitulation to the current humanism is nevertheless quite obvious at a number of points and its roots undoubtedly reach down into his attitude toward nature. He is opposed to thinking that God miraculously interposes in the natural workings of the world and suggests that Christ should be seen, not as a divine being who became enfleshed at Nazareth, but as a human whose divine significance lies principally in the minds of his biographers and who through his life affirms the validity of ours. Küng is strongly opposed to the Anselmian doctrine of satisfaction, of Christ at the cross doing for man what in his helpless and debt-ridden state man could not do for himself. This, says Küng, is to be opposed because it is impersonal and because it depends upon a notion of judicial equivalence. Furthermore, it rests on the notion that there was once a paradise as well as a primal pair out of which the human race sprang and to which the sin from the original fall was transmitted. This, he believes, is all very questionable. Küng acknowledges that the New Testament utilizes sacrificial imagery and substitutionary terminology to speak of Christ's death. Today, however, this is best translated into the notions of representation and of God identifying with man in his fallen state. Salvation is, therefore, thought of as 'humanization' in much the same way as it is in Bonhoeffer and some of the secular theologians.

Küng's new *summa,* then, hardly makes reference to justification, denies its theological antecedents in the penal doctrines of sin and the vicarious, substitutionary atonement of Christ, compromises the kind of christology that is required by this doctrine and overlooks entirely the place of preaching the biblical Word as a means of eliciting the

151

sinner's faith in such an act of objective redemption.[33] It may be argued that this represents a new position for him; it is more likely that his former study on justification was a theological exercise which did not expose clearly some of the vital, underlying assumptions in his thinking. Robert Jenson was almost alone in perceiving this, remarking that he doubted whether the Swiss theologian had any conception of Luther's agonies as he searched for the gracious God;[34] still less, it is apparent, did Küng really understand how Luther's *Angst* was resolved.

Contrary to what one might have expected from reading Küng's first book, the Second Vatican Council did not have much occasion to endorse Reformation themes.[35] It produced some eloquent descriptions of the horizontal effects of sin, but the vertical dimension, the effect of sin on the divine-human relationship, was weak. Sin was described as 'imbalance'. Consequently man was exhorted to use his freedom to emancipate himself from sinful passions and return to God. Man does not, of course, have full freedom to do this — that would be Pelagianism — so he does need the help of grace by which he can 'bring such a relationship with God into full flower'.[36] It is difficult to see how this teaching avoids synergism. Man and God in Küng's phrase do, indeed, seem to be pulling on the same rope.

The word *grace* was hardly if ever used to describe God's unmerited favour in forgiving men through Christ. It was used, rather, as a synonym for divine life, gifts or help, for those realities which are even in the atheist's heart and which lie behind his good works.[37] It is grace in these other senses which inspires virginity,[38] comes in the sacraments[39] and produces holy living. The word *justification* was used twice.[40] The one instance was a reiteration of Roman 4:25 which was not exegeted at all. The other was the simple statement that justification comes by faith through baptism. Salvation, in fact, is through the sacraments.[41] In the eucharist, 'the Victim' is offered to God[42] and grace in turn is derived from the elements. Regeneration is through baptism, pardon through penance, and martyrdom is the means of being transformed into the Master's image by the voluntary shedding of blood.[43]

References to the cross and the 'paschal mystery' are numerous in some documents but surprisingly absent from others. In terms of the traditional typing of atonement theories, they are not particularly

152

explicit although they seem to be dominated by the classic motif and the subjective, mystical theory. The classic emerges in phrases such as 'dying he destroyed our death and, rising, he restored our life', or that he overcame 'death through his own death and resurrection'.[44] The mystical theory is more often assumed than stated, but a striking affirmation is given in *Gaudium et spes:* 'For by his incarnation the Son of God has united Himself in some fashion with every man.'[45] The Latin view is represented in its Anselmian expression in such expressions as that 'he *merited* [my italics] life for us by the free shedding of his own blood'.[46] This is apparently the idea of Christ as the Ultimate Penitent doing absolutely and completely for us what we can only do partially and relatively for ourselves, namely offer reparation for our sins. The idea of substitution is present but not, it would seem, in the Pauline sense of Christ standing in the sinner's stead and himself bearing the sinner's punishment. Here the direction is upward; man, in and through Christ, reaches up to God by penitence. In the New Testament the direction is downward; God, in and through Christ, reaches down to man by bearing his penalty and forgiving him.

Evaluation

It would seem clear enough that the traditional soteriological structure, whose centre is the difference between but the continuing relation of nature and grace, has continued into contemporary Catholic thought. The reflection of the last two decades which was mostly assumed if not explicitly endorsed by the Council has served merely to refine this rather than to correct it.[47] Within an acceptance of the older ideas, the divine initiative in saving men has been more heavily underscored than before, though not to the exclusion of some human co-operation. Likewise, the more legalistic understanding of faith has given way to the *existentiell* concern with active participation and finding the full potential of human personhood. Important aspects of the biblical notion of faith have, in the process, been recovered but there is still a question mark over what it is that is being believed for salvation.

The invincibility of both the nature-grace correlation and the inherited sacramental system is seen most plainly in the efforts of the charismatic theologians to reconcile their Catholic faith with their experience of being baptized in the Spirit. Theoretically, grace has been infused slowly into nature; experientially, it has come suddenly, dramatically, at a specific point in time. Can theory and experience be reconciled? Those scholars who have worked at all with the problem have chosen more or less unanimously to interpret the experience in the light of the theory rather than modifying the theory in the light of the experience. There are, of course, differences in the way this has been achieved. But a consensus seems to be emerging that theory and experience should be seen as the two sides of the same coin. That grace which was given objectively in the sacraments came to be realized subjectively in the 'baptism of the Spirit'. Entry into the Roman Church results in the giving of the Spirit, especially in the sacraments, but there is a time lag before this gift is actually experienced. The later manifestation of the Spirit and his 'reviviscence' in the individual's life is what makes dogma come alive and what enables the individual to experience its verities subjectively.[48] The interior renewal thus takes place within an acceptance of traditional teaching.

To say that the nature-grace correlation has remained intact is not, of course, to deny that there has, in recent decades, been an evolution in Catholic belief. With respect to salvation, this has been evident in at least five important areas. First, the 'biblical revival' has injected a new interest in scriptural teaching into current theology; indeed, warnings have occasionally been issued about the dangers of drifting into an arid kind of fundamentalism. This would seem to be unlikely since the traditional Catholic doctrine of inspiration is under fire at present and in the Church at large little Bible reading is actually being done.[49] Yet the result has been to clothe theology in more chaste and biblical terms. Secondly, there has been a greater concern to emphasize God's initiative in grace, which undoubtedly reiterates a biblical emphasis. Thirdly, the desire to see the sacraments as functioning in a less wooden, mechanistic way is laudable. The older belief in their *ex opere operato* performance had the effect of virtually eliminating the place of personal appropriation by faith. Fourthly, the effect of personalism has been to draw attention to the subjective side of Christian belief which was often underplayed in the periods of high orthodoxy. Consequently, the experiencing person is now firmly ensconced on one end of any formulation of the meaning of faith.

Finally, the reinterpretation of the *extra ecclesiam nulla salus* formula — however questionable the means by which it was accomplished — has removed an obstacle to a more biblical perception of salvation. Undoubtedly the church has an important role to play but it would seem that Scripture never pictures this in terms of an intermediary between Christ and the sinner.

These are all solid gains but they have not affected to any significant degree the soteriological core, the nature-grace correlation[50] in which all men are in a state of grace though the grace may not be active. Is it right, then, to think of nature as being soteriologically directed and sustained by grace outside of the faith-acceptance of Christ's act of justification in his cross-work? Is grace, either in the traditional sense of sanctifying grace or in its modification through the supernatural existential, a universal phenomenon common to all men? Did the fall extinguish completely or merely diminish partially the inward openness to God? Is man fallen and captive to sin through his rebellion against God or is he merely in a state of imbalance through sin and therefore able in part to co-operate with grace?

It is difficult to see how Rahner and Küng can validly argue that the Reformers' views on these questions are essentially the same as those of contemporary Catholicism when the outlook of contemporary Catholicism with its nature-grace correlation is, but for some minor refinements, precisely what Luther and the other Reformers rejected in the Catholicism of their day.[51]

According to Luther, the nature-grace correlation rested on the Aristotelian theory of virtue. This posited that men are equipped by nature to be virtuous and what is required is simply that the ethical ability be exercised and trained. When transported into the realm of theology, this resulted in the teaching of salvation by slow ascent in which 'works' — the personal response to inward, sanctifying grace — played a part in the person's acceptance before God. The ascent's precise steps and their appropriate order were debated in scholasticism. Most commonly, however, the first was seen to be the infusion of grace into nature, to be followed, secondly, by the necessary moral co-operation, resulting, thirdly, in the expectation of eternal life as a just recompense. Given this understanding of nature and grace, it can be said that no good work ever results without grace. Grace is the prime mover of the religious life. And with this, Luther had no

155

quarrel. He did, however, take exception to the idea that salvation should be seen as the outcome and just reward for the co-operation given to grace. As often as good works might be ascribed solely to grace, grace was not the sole cause of salvation, for human co-operation with grace was an ingredient in the process of being progressively justified.

To say, as has often been said, that Catholics believed in the necessity of good works and Protestants in the indispensability of grace is, therefore, a piece of *haute vulgarisation* which simply clouds the issues. It was more complex than that.

The issue really boiled down to whether unregenerate nature – the 'natural man' in Paul's terminology – has the intrinsic freedom to respond to grace and the innate ability to free itself, however partially, from sinful passion. This was the issue Luther and Erasmus debated in 1524 and 1525. Addressing Erasmus, Luther declared that 'you alone, in contrast with all others, have attacked the real thing, that is, the essential issue.' In comparison to this, the papacy, purgatory and indulgences are 'trifles, rather than issues'. This question Luther described as 'the hinge on which all turns', this is 'the vital spot'.[52]

Indeed, he had seen this before he had posted his theses and some time before the definitive writings and events of 1520. In his 'Disputation against Scholastic Theology', defended on 4 September 1517, he declared that it is false 'to state that man's inclination is free to choose between either of two opposites.... The inclination is not free, but captive.'[53] The will is as bad as the nature of which it is a part; it is, therefore, 'innately and inevitably evil and corrupt'.[54] To argue that salvation could depend in any way on man's response to and co-operation with grace was, to Luther, preposterous. 'On the part of man,' he declared, 'nothing precedes grace except ill will and even rebellion against grace.'[55] Later, he went on to say that all such efforts at co-operation resulted only in damnable, mortal sin.

This position was aptly summarized by Luther's co-worker, Philip Melanchthon, thus: 'The miserable human heart stands like a desolate, deserted, old and decaying house, God no longer dwelling within and winds blowing through. That is, all sorts of conflicting tendencies and lusts drive the heart to the manifold sins of uncontrolled love, hate, envy, and pride.... When we speak about this great ruin of human powers, we are not talking about free will, for man's will and heart are wretchedly imprisoned, impaired, and ruined, so that inwardly man's heart and will are unlike the divine law, offensive and hostile to it, and man cannot by his own inward natural powers be obedient.'[56] This conviction became the cornerstone of the Reformation soteriology, being affirmed additionally by Calvin, Bucer, Cranmer, Knox and Zwingli. It was expressed catechetically, liturgically, and credally.

The Reformers, without exception, replaced the nature-grace model by two other distinctions which they believed to be more biblical. First, they distinguished between natural and supernatural revelation. The former, which is common to all, is a knowledge of God's existence and the moral nature of human life; the latter is peculiar to those who in the Word, written and living, come to see and know God. It becomes, through the Spirit's recreative work within the soul, a saving revelation. Natural revelation, unlike sanctifying grace, cannot provide a basis on which man can be saved although it is the backdrop to his salvation. Secondly, they distinguished between law and gospel. If the language was peculiarly Luther's, the idea was common to them all. The law was given, not to show that man can co-operate with grace, but to show that he cannot. It reveals that his captivity to sin is humanly unbreakable and that his rebellion against God is incorrigible. It exposes his inability and this exposure is the only adequate preparation for the reception of the gospel. Consequently, Luther sundered apart faith and works. In his conception, works, or the volitional response to grace, never have anything but an horizontal dimension and faith alone is given a vertical direction, operating through the Word and Spirit. There is no salvation by slow, volitional ascent. The issue was not whether by co-operating with grace nature could be perfected, but whether the promises of God of forgiveness through Jesus' justifying death could be believed.

If the Protestant Reformers were even approximately correct in their understanding of Christian salvation, two concluding observations need to be made about contemporary Catholicism. First, its doctrine of sin is weak and insufficiently developed. It is from this deficiency that the nature-grace doctrine arises; from the nature-grace doctrine flows the rest of the soteriology, the inescapable outcome of which is that works, in the sense of volitional co-operation, play a part in salvation. This is at odds with the biblical outlook. Secondly, the doctrine of the universal presence of grace is in the future almost certainly going to lead into universalism.[57] The tendency toward universalism has always been checked by the notion that outside the Church there is no salvation. As this check has crumbled,[58] the latent tendency toward universalism has emerged in many ways, not least in the new, benevolent attitude toward non-Christian religions and atheists. However difficult Christian particularism is to maintain, there is no question that it accords with what Jesus and the apostles taught as recorded in Scripture.

The outward changes in the Church's structure, its worship, its practices and general style of religious life have in many ways been refreshing. Older differences have been laid to rest and a common search for biblical truth has been made more simple. On the other hand, the underlying Pelagian tendencies from the past have not been reformed. And in turn these have blossomed into a humanism which, if it is religious in its outlook, is increasingly less ecclesiastical and more comfortably secular. The price of such acceptance must inevitably be a further alienation from the content of biblical faith.

Notes

[1] The Catholic doctrine of grace is complex. Traditionally, there have been several divisions and distinctions in the doctrine, such as the following: (i) Uncreated and created grace. Uncreated grace refers to those special benefits of grace arising from the incarnation, the indwelling of God in the soul and a person's final possession by God in the beatific vision. Created grace, by contrast, refers to a general gift, common to all men, which gives them a sense of the divine and therefore precedes union with him. (ii) External and internal grace. The former has to do mainly with deeds and events whose effects are moral, such as sermons, liturgy and the example of the saints; revelation and the sacraments have also been included in this category. The latter are those mysterious, internal influences on the soul such as sanctifying grace, infused virtues and actual grace. (iii) Habitual and actual grace. Habitual grace is another term for sanctifying grace when worked out in the life. It refers to the internalized, supernatural quality given at baptism as a result of which a person later becomes justified. Actual grace is God's periodic intervention in stirring up and sustaining sanctifying grace. This occurs through the enlightenment of the intellect, the disposing and sustaining of the will and the general capacity to do saving acts. See Ludwig Ott, *Fundamentals of Catholic Dogma* (St Louis, 1964), pp. 219–269. On the early history of the doctrine of grace, see Henri Rondet, *The Grace of Christ* (Westminster, 1967), pp. 199–204, which briefly delineates the main lines of its treatment.

[2] For the key points of this conception see Henry Denzinger, *The Sources of Catholic Dogma* (London, 1955), pp. 1295, 1356–1358, 177–181, 105, 130, 317, 325, 800–802, 833–843.

[3] The new concern with formulating Christian faith from within the human situation is well exhibited, for example, in *Concilium*, 19, *Spirituality in the Secular City*, ed. Christian Dugnoc (New York, 1966). Of special note are the essays by Michael de Certeau, 'Culture and Spiritual Experience' (pp. 3–31); Robert Bultot, 'The Theology of Earthly Realities and Lay Spirituality' (pp. 44–58); Claude J. Geffré, 'Desacralization and the Spiritual Life' (pp. 111–131). See also Karl Rahner, 'Theological Reflections on the Problem of Secularization', *Renewal of Religious Thought*, ed. L. K. Shock (3 vols.; Montreal, 1968), I, pp. 167–192.

[4] See J. Hyde, 'Grace: a Bibliographical Note', *Irish Theological Quarterly*, 32 (July 1965), pp. 257–261; Eugene Teselle, 'Nature and Grace in the Forum of Ecumenical Discussion', *Journal of Ecumenical Studies* (Summer 1971), pp. 539–559; Francis Colborn, 'The Theology of Grace: Present Trends and Future Directions', *Theological Studies*, 31 (December 1970), pp. 692–711.

[5] Pius XII's important encyclical, *Humani generis* (1950) rejected the possibility of distinguishing between form and content in dogma, although Pope John XXIII gave a cautious blessing to the distinction in his address to the Second Vatican Council. See G. C. Berkouwer, *The Second Vatican Council and the New Catholicism* (Grand Rapids, 1965), pp. 82–88.

[6] An excellent if optimistic summary of the efforts to work out the ideas of development is found in Mark Schoof, *A Survey of Catholic Theology 1800–1970* (New York, 1970), pp. 157–227; Owen Chadwick, *From Bossuet to Newman: The Idea of Doctrinal Development* (Cambridge, 1957); Karl Rahner, *Theological Investigations* (10 vols., London and Baltimore, 1961–67), IV, pp. 3–35.

[7] The word *nature* is used in several different ways, the main ones being: (i) that which underlies the many bodily changes which take place and which provides self-identity through the years of a person's life; (ii) man considered as he was originally in his inward nature, in which there was, by God's grace, complete harmony; (iii) man inwardly considered as enslaved to his own ego and sinful desires and therefore unable to reach his destiny; (iv) man's interior life seen as damaged by sin but benefiting from the slow reparation of redeeming grace.

[8] For a summary of the relationship between nature and grace in traditional theology see Karl Rahner, *Nature and Grace: Dilemmas in the Modern Church* (London, 1963: New York, 1964), pp. 114–149; see also his *Theological Investigations*, I, pp. 297–318.

[9] Process theology, however, comes close to destroying God's freedom in grace, as is seen, for example, in the studies by Gregory Baum, especially *Man Becoming: God in Secular Language* (New York, 1970). See Norman L. Geisler, 'Process Theology', *Tensions in Contemporary Theology*, ed. Stanley N. Gundry and Alan F. Johnson (Chicago, 1976), pp. 237–286.

[10] See J. P. Kenny, 'Supernatural Existential', *New Catholic Encyclopedia*, XIII, pp. 816, 817; J. P. Kenny, 'Reflections on Human Nature and the Supernatural', *Theological Studies*, 14 (1953), pp. 280–287.

[11] On Rahner's theory, in its broad setting, see Louis Roberts, *The Achievement of Karl Rahner* (New York, 1967), pp. 122–223. R. Bechtie, 'Karl Rahner's Supernatural Existential: A Personalistic Approach', *Thought*. 28 (September 1973). pp. 61–77.

[12] Edward Schillebeeckx, *Revelation and Theology* (2 vols.; London, 1967: New York, 1968), II, pp. 128–133. *Cf.* Edward Bozzo, 'The Neglected Dimension: Grace in Interpersonal Context', *Theological Studies*, 29 (1968), pp. 497–504. The personalist approach is developed also in James Mackey's *The Grace of God, The Response of Man* (Albany, 1966).

[13] Max Seckler, *Instinkt und Glaubenseville* (Mainz, 1961).

[14] The Second Vatican Council, in its Dogmatic Constitution on Divine Revelation, similarly used the word *revelation* in two senses. It is used of propositional truths which result from inspiration, or of the subjective act of revealing by the Spirit. See George H. Tavard, *The Dogmatic Constitution on Divine Revelation of Vatican Council II, Promulgated by Pope Paul VI, November 18, 1965 – Commentary and Translation* (London, 1966), pp. 17ff.; B. C. Butler, *The Theology of Vatican II* (London, 1967), pp. 28–58.

[15] *Decl. Ch. Non-Chr. Rel.*, p. 1.

[16] *Ibid.*, p. 2. Culture, the Council allowed, might 'serve as a guidance course toward the true God, or as a preparation for the gospel'. *Dec. Miss. Act*, p. 3. On this basis, Pope John XXIII in his *Pacem in terris* declared that there was good in Marxism; this, too, is the basis for the ongoing Christian-Marxist dialogue.

[17] *Const. Ch.*, p. 16; *Dec. Miss. Act.*, p. 16; *Const. Ch. World*, p. 16.

[18] Thomas F. Stransky, 'The Declaration on Non-Christian Religions', *Vatican II: An Interfaith Appraisal*, ed. John H. Miller (Notre Dame, 1966), p.341. *Cf.* Rahner, *Theological Investigations*, V, pp.115–134.

[19] See Rahner, *Theological Investigations*, VI, pp. 390–398; Klaus Riesenhuber, 'Rahner's Anonymous Christian', *Theological Digest*, 13 (Fall, 1965), pp. 163–171; Eugene Hillman, 'Anonymous Christianity and the Missions', *Downside Review*, 84 (1966), pp. 361–379. The theme is developed by Anita Röper in *The Anonymous Christians*, and its relation to the church by Richard P. McBrien, *Do We Need The Church?* (New York, 1966).

[20] Careful documentation is provided for these views in J. J. King, *The Necessity of the Church for Salvation in Selected Theological Writings of the Past Century* (Washington, 1960).

[21] The translated text may be found in *American Ecclesiastical Review*, 127, No. 4 (October 1952), pp. 307–315.

[22] Congar's argument is largely in agreement with Jean Daniélou, *The Salvation of the Nations* (Notre Dame, 1962) but Congar is somewhat critical of Riccardo Lombardi's *The Salvation of the Unbeliever* in which it is argued, on the basis of Scripture's 'universal' texts, that what is necessary for salvation by way of objective belief is in the possession of almost all people.

[23] Rahner, *Theological Investigations*, II, pp. 1–88. This means, says Butler, commenting on the conciliar text, that in men of all religions as well as in men of no religion, 'Christ is (anonymously) at work and . . . in them, the Church *extra quam nulla salus*, is transcending her own visible limits' (p. 167). It is a view that clearly depends on a distinction between the visible and invisible church, a distinction which used to be dismissed as heretical. *Cf.* Hans Küng, *The Church* (New York, 1967), pp. 34–39.

[24] *Const. Ch.*, p. 14.

[25] *Ibid.*, pp. 14, 15, 16.

[26] *Cf.* the brief study by Joseph Fichtner, *Theological Anthropology: The Science of Man in his Relations to God* (Notre Dame, 1963).

[27] Richard Stauffer, *Luther as Seen by Catholics* (London, 1967).

[28] Hans Küng, *Infallible? An Inquiry* (London and New York, 1971). See John J. Kirvan, ed., *The Infallibility Debate* (New York, 1971).

[29] Hubert Jedin, *A History of the Council of Trent* (2 vols., St Louis, 1957–).

[30] Hans Küng, *Justification: The Doctrine of Karl Barth and a Catholic Reflection* (New York, 1964: London, 1966). Rahner, commenting on Küng's work, declares that there 'is no reason for doubting the orthodoxy of the general presentation of the Catholic doctrine of justification', which, he says, is also attested by Bouyer, de Broglie and Ebneter. 'His point', Rahner goes on, 'is to show that those very truths which Barth finds lacking in the Catholic position are actually held in it, the truths which he declares must never be given up if the gospel is to be maintained.' Rahner, *Theological Investigations*, IV, p. 190.

[31] Küng, *Justification*, p. 230. The differences between the Reformation view of justification *sola gratia, sola fideo*, and the Catholic view, Rahner also declares to be 'purely verbal'. Both sides can see today that grace and freedom are entities that grow in the same proportion, not in inverse proportion; that justifying faith is in fact the individual's firm hope of salvation; that faith which attains the complete fulfilment of its nature in total self-surrender to God is that charity which makes faith justifying faith. Karl Rahner and Herbert Vorgrimler, *Concise Theological Dictionary* (London and New York, 1965), pp. 173, 174. The issues as formulated in the

sixteenth century emerge clearly through a comparison of the Tridentine decrees with the Protestant responses, although it should be noted that the Protestants were not privy to the many private discussions that lay behind the conciliar statements. See John Calvin, *Tracts*, ed. Henry Beveridge (3 vols.; Edinburgh, 1851), III, pp. 108–162; Martin Chemnitz, *Examination of the Council of Trent, Part 1* (St Louis, 1971), pp. 465–544.

[32] The notion of the supernatural existential is treated briefly by Küng – 'It would take the equivalent of a book to develop conceptually the theological implications of the autological presence of the whole creation in Jesus Christ, so this must be omitted here' (p. 141) – as is christology. He argues that creation by Christ guarantees a supernatural ethos to the natural order. There are 'different stages' of relationship, so 'being in Jesus Christ is not simply identical with being just' (p. 145). This coincides precisely with Rahner's view.

[33] The same weakness is evident in Rahner. See his 'Demythologization and the Sermon', *Concilium*, 33, *The Renewal of Preaching, Theory and Practice* (New York, 1968), pp. 20–38.

[34] See Robert W. Jenson's review of Küng's book in *Dialog*, V (Summer 1966), p. 232.

[35] American Catholic laity, while they do not present in microcosm the rest of the world, are of interest to religious sociologists because of the relatively high degree of literacy and high level of mass media communication which they absorb. At about the time the council was meeting, however, Reformation themes were not very evident among them. In 1968, only 26% had 'any sense of being saved in Christ'. Amongst the main prerequisites of salvation cited were baptism (65%), doing good (65%), prayer (54%) and belief in Christ as Saviour (54%). Rodney Stark and Charles Y. Glock, *American Piety: The Nature of Religious Commitment* (Berkeley, 1968), pp. 43, 44.

[36] *Const. Ch.*, p. 17.

[37] *Ibid.*

[38] *Ibid.*, p. 42.

[39] *Ibid.*, p. 41.

[40] *Dec. Chr. Ed.*, p. 3; *Const. Ch.*, p. 9.

[41] *Ibid.*, p. 28.

[42] *Ibid.*

[43] *Ibid.*, p. 42.

[44] *Const. Ch.*, p. 7.

[45] *Const. Ch. World*, p. 3.

[46] *Ibid.*, p. 22.

[47] The most striking indication that the fundamental structure of grace was untouched by the Council was its refusal to change any mariological tenet. To Barth, this is the one 'heresy' that explains all the others for here we find the 'type and essence of the human creature co-operating servantlike (*ministerialiter*) in its own redemption on the basis of prevenient grace' (Barth, *Church Dogmatics*, I, 2, p. 143). See my *Revolution in Rome* (Downers Grove, 1972: London, 1973). pp. 129–137.

[48] General descriptions of the Catholic charismatic movement can be found in Edward D. O'Connor, *The Pentecostal Movement in the Catholic Church* (Notre Dame, 1971), and Kevin and Dorothy Ranaghan, *Catholic Pentecostals* (Paramus, 1969). Suggestions for theological interpretation are found in Donald L. Gelpi, *Pentecostalism: A Theological Viewpoint* (Paramus, 1971) and Kilian McDonnell's paper, 'A Statement of the Theological Basis of the Catholic Charismatic Renewal', read at the 1973 International Congress in Rome and reprinted in *Review for Religions*, 33 (March 1974), pp. 344–352.

[49] Several pieces of unrelated sociological analysis on American Catholics indicate this. Since the surveys were conducted by different researchers in different areas, the figures need to be treated with caution. Yet it is not insignificant that in a country with high literacy levels, those doing daily Bible reading declined from 15% in 1952 to 2% in 1968. Those who never read the

Bible at all rose from 25% in 1952 to 53% in 1968. Martin E. Marty, Stuart E. Rosenburg, and Andrew Greeley, *What Do We Believe?* (New York, 1968), p. 230; Stark and Glock, p. 110.

[50] Karl Rahner has outlined the scholastic understanding of the relation between created and uncreated grace, pointing out that however 'diverse they may be among themselves, it is true of all the scholastic theories that they see God's indwelling and his conjunction with the justified man as based exclusively upon created grace' (*Theological Investigations*, I, p. 324). Created grace, what is given to man *as man*, is the basis on which his justification is erected. This, Rahner believes, is compatible with Scripture, and he approves of Küng's study. In simple language, de Lubac says: 'Christ did not come to take our place – or rather this aspect of substitution refers only to the first stage of his work – but to enable us to raise ourselves through him to God. . . . Humanity was to co-operate actively in its own salvation, and that is why to the act of his sacrifice Christ joined the objective revelation of his Person and the foundation of his Church.' Henri de Lubac, *Catholicism: Christ and the Common Destiny of Man* (London, 1950), pp. 113, 114.

[51] Luther's relationship to medieval scholasticism is well if briefly explicated in Steven E. Ozment, 'Homo Viator: Luther and Late Medieval Theology', *Harvard Theological Review*, 62, No. 3 (1969), pp. 275–288, some of the same points emerging in his *Homo Spiritualis: A Comparative Study of the Anthropology of Tauler, Gerson and Luther 1509–16* (Leiden, 1969).

[52] Martin Luther, *The Bondage of the Will* (London and Westwood, 1957), p. 319. The subsequent attempts to show that Luther changed his mind on this subject are not convincing. *Cf.* Chemnitz, pp. 413–453.

[53] Martin Luther, *Luther's Works; Career of the Reformer*, 1, ed. Harold J. Grimm (55 vols.; Philadelphia, 1957), XXXI, p. 9.

[54] *Ibid.*, p. 10.

[55] *Ibid.*, p. 11.

[56] Philip Melanchthon, *Melanchthon on Christian Doctrine: Loci Communes 1955*, ed. Clyde L. Manschreck (Oxford, 1965), p. 52.

[57] The possibility of universalism, if unchecked, is present even in the words of so cautious and conservative a spokesman as Pope Paul VI. It is 'God's will to save all men', he recently declared. All are 'called to a higher destiny made accessible by Christ, all potentially sons of God and brothers, all invited to the same salvation. . . . It is an amazing and grandiose vision of the humanity and mercy of God.' He went on to add, however, that such a vision should lead to fresh missionary activity, for as yet the Catholic Church is universal in name but not in reality. Pope Paul VI, 'Oct. 22, 1967: Message to the Whole Church about the Universality of Salvation', *Christ to the World*, 13, No. 2 (1968), p. 105.

[58] In the United States, attendance at Mass between 1964 and 1974 dropped from 71% to 50%, monthly confession from 38% to 17%, belief in Peter's founding of the Roman Church from 70% to 42%, and in 1974 those who believed in papal infallibility under the circumstances described at Vatican I had fallen to 32%. Shirley Saldahna *et al.*, 'American Catholics – Ten Years Later', *The Critic*, 33 (January–February 1975), p. 17.

Ask, and it will be given to you; seek, and you will find; knock, and it will be opened to you. For every one who asks receives, and he who seeks finds, and to him who knocks it will be opened.

Matthew 7:7, 8

For the word of the cross is folly to those who are perishing, but to us who are being saved it is the power of God. . . . The foolishness of God is wiser than men, and the weakness of God is stronger than men.

1 Corinthians 1:18, 25

Examine yourselves, to see whether you are holding to your faith. Test yourselves.

2 Corinthians 13:5a

Chapter Seven

Conclusion

Different as the theologies under discussion have been, they have all started from a common problem. It is the problem of how to be Christian in a secular age. How can Christian faith remain true to itself if it is speaking to the world in a way that is comprehensible to that world?

There has, of course, always been a chasm that has separated the believer's view of life from the unbeliever's. Often, however, the depth of this chasm has been obscured by the fact that western culture has borrowed as much from Christian faith as from scepticism. The institution of government, the understanding of law, the rights of the person, the practice of the arts, the place of the family and the role of education in most western nations have been formed by both belief and unbelief. That common territory, however, is now disappearing rapidly. Brunner is undoubtedly right in saying that this is the first time a major civilization has sought to build itself, self-consciously and deliberately, without religious foundations. For many people there is no acknowledged supernatural order lying behind the social fabric. Government, law, the arts and education are now increasingly accountable, not to a higher order, but to themselves alone, and the secular person sees these constituents of his life simply as ends in themselves. 'God' is not relevant to what he does each day, nor is he accountable to 'God' for what he does. Given this prevailing mindset, Christian theology is faced with a profound problem in communication.

It is the recognition of this fact that has turned theology away from its strictly dogmatic concerns towards apologetic interests. The movement began in earnest with the 'father of modern theology', Friedrich Schleiermacher, especially in his *Religion: Speeches to its Cultured Despisers* (1799). Acutely sensitive to the shifting intellectual patterns as a result of which Christian faith was becoming irrelevant,

Schleiermacher struggled valiantly to find a new place for it in the modern world. To a marked degree he succeeded, but he did so by yielding the older Christian insistence on a saving revelation from a God essentially outside of this world's time-frame who has penetrated into it in the person of the Son. In place of this, he substituted an understanding constructed largely from within the flux of human experience. The assumptions of the Enlightened new world were hardly violated by this, but the question which he left behind and which has continued to haunt his variegated posterity to this day is how well he also succeeded in preserving an authentic Christian faith.

In retrospect, it is now clear that theology came to a point of decision in Schleiermacher, the consequences of which are evident throughout the expositions that have filled these pages. Is theology and in particular the doctrine of salvation to be written in terms of modern self-understanding, or is it to be written in terms of God's revelation in Scripture? The existential, secular and liberation theologies have clearly developed within the bounds of modern self-consciousness and as such are *apologetic* ventures. On the other side of the question there is conservative theology which is the most obvious *dogmatic* theology. Both neo-orthodoxy and Catholic theology are mediating positions assuming into a synthesis both dogmatic and apologetic elements. Dogmatic theologies always struggle with the question as to how, as expositions of the supernatural Word, they can root themselves in the contemporary age; apologetic theologies are always vulnerable to the charge that the extent to which they are compatible with modern self-consciousness is the extent to which they have ceased to be Christian.

The different starting points of these two groups of theologies, their different purposes and different ways of working are evident in the tensions which have been examined throughout these pages but which crystallize into three fundamental questions. First, is the saving God immanent or transcendent? Secondly, is salvation subjective or objective? Thirdly, is it personal or corporate?

Is God immanent or transcendent?

The first question concerns God's relationship to human existence. Is he wholly domiciled within it or is he also apart from and above it?

Put in this form, the question seems to force a false option, for it is clear to most theologians that the extremes of nullifying immanence by an exaggerated transcendence or transcendence by an exaggerated immanence are alike aberrations. On the one hand, God must be related to the world in ways beyond merely a first act of creation; on the other hand, he cannot be so identified with the world that it becomes deified and he is entrapped within it. In both cases God's effective power over and within the world is destroyed, and in the latter, man's humanity and God's divinity, in merging into a *tertium quid*, mutually contaminate and so destroy one another.

Seeing the dangers inherent in these one-sided solutions, as most theologians have, has not itself been enough. For a good case can be made for saying that those theologies that are working from within modern self-experience have found it impossible to arrive at an adequate conception of transcendence. The reason for this is that the biblical notion of transcendence, as Kenneth Hamilton has rightly argued, is tied into a supernatural world-view, and it is precisely this that is incomprehensible to and incompatible with the assumptions to which these theologies have wedded themselves. Divine transcendence has to be denied or profoundly modified if these theologies are to seem to be apologetically valid.

The distinction between what is 'natural' and what is 'supernatural' was, of course, originally scholastic, but the idea is everywhere present in the Bible. There is no need to posit that its authors believed in two-layered cakes and triple-decker buses, a God 'above' and hell 'below'. Spatial images were used but not with this degree of literalness. No biblical author ever imagined that God is secluded in an ethereal realm far above the earth from which he might periodically take a journey and visit his creation. Nor is there any need to endorse some of the justifications for miracles which seemed to give credence to this caricature. God is not a cosmic Viking who periodically decides to make a raid on nature but unfortunately always escapes without ever being seen, leaving behind him only the strewn wreckage of what were once orderly 'laws of nature'. On the contrary, God is everywhere present in the world (Is. 66:1; Acts 7:48, 49), and it derives its continuing existence from him (Ps. 139:7–10; Acts 17:27, 28). Yet God is separate from it and especially from its focal peak, man. He is separate by reason of his being, holiness, wrath and glory

167

(Ps. 102:26, 27; Is. 40:25; Ex. 15:11; Is. 10:5, 6; Hab. 1:13–17; Is. 42:8; Ex. 33:18–23). And the fact that he is not captive to his creation, that he is not bound by its workings, is plain from the miracles Scripture records. These miracles, which are exhibitions of great power and productive of great wonder, reveal God's activity in the world in ways out of the ordinary, when the 'laws of nature' are temporarily suspended.

When we speak of God as being transcendent, then, we are affirming a supernatural world-view in which God works in ways that are extraordinary (miracles) as well as ordinary (the observed uniformities of nature's workings), in which he is free from the world even while he sustains it, in which he remains infinite even while he relates to what is finite. Within this conception, God is ontologically different from man, although man remains in God's image. God continues to be morally pure despite his relation with sinful people. And this, it would seem, is the context in which Scripture speaks of the *agapē*-God taking action within human life, not naturally but supernaturally, to overturn at the cross man's thraldom to sin, guilt and the hosts of wickedness.

It is this supernatural cosmology, however, which is offensive to the post-Enlightenment world. A number of the theologies we have surveyed have correspondingly argued that its preservation is unnecessary to the continuance of Christian faith. This does not mean, however, that the concept of transcendence is simply abandoned; what happens is that it is redefined, often by means of contemporary philosophical notions.

The correspondence of the new terms to the old is not, however, precise. In a supernatural framework, the idea of divine transcendence has one meaning; in a philosophical framework, the idea of the Absolute (which is its supposed equivalent) has a very different meaning. The old notion of a transcendent God had reference to a reality partly *outside* of and above human experience, but this has been replaced by a point of reference wholly *within* human experience. The Absolute, the philosophical substitute for the Transcendent, is often identified with the sense of mystery, with the central intuitive insight, or the controlling 'religious' perception which a theologian has. And this sense, insight and perception becomes a reference point in accordance with which the whole body of theological truth is rewritten.

168

There are, as a result, two entirely different conceptions of God, depending on whether one is reading a dogmatic theology whose first concern is to receive the teaching of Scripture within its own cosmology or an apologetic theology whose opening manoeuvre is to start building its affirmations on presuppositions about reality which are shared with secular contemporaries. Not only are there two Gods but two Christs, two gospels, two schemes of salvation, two views of man and two understandings of the world. Whether a person opts for a dogmatic or an apologetic theology will always be determined at the level of presuppositions, many of which may be unexamined or even unrecognized.

Is salvation subjective or objective?

The second question over which there is a sharp division is whether salvation is subjective or objective. Once again, this would seem to pose a false option, for, in so far as the teaching of Christ has any relevance to the Christian today; it has an 'objective' element, and in so far as the Christian today is an experiencing subject, his belief must have a 'subjective' element. But it is in asking how Jesus' work and teaching are relevant and how they are experienced as such that the differences show up and Christian opinion begins to cluster around the two poles.

At one end are those schemes which, by an unchecked application of the classic theory, have almost obviated the need for the subjective appropriation of Christ's saving work. These include neo-orthodoxy, the liberation theologies and some parts of Roman Catholicism. On the other end, are the existential and secular theologies which have focused decisively on subjective consciousness to the point of negating the significance of the objective elements of Christ's life, death and resurrection. The interesting fact to note, however, is that universalism is presupposed, albeit for different reasons, both by those whose interests are predominantly subjective as well as by those whose orientation is objective. It articulates easily with both types of theological structure. Conservative theology is almost alone in insisting that the objective and subjective elements of Christian faith cannot be diluted.

169

It is rooted in the historical life and death of Christ through whom sin and guilt are decisively cancelled, but this event is made personal by the inner work of the Spirit and the obedient response of faith. The objective and subjective aspects correlate well with the insistence of conservative theology that reality is both natural and supernatural, that God is both immanent and transcendent.

Is salvation personal or corporate?

There are basically two ways by which a theology comes to view faith as personal. Either, as in the case of conservative theology, there is the basis of the Latin view of the atonement, or there is the intrusion of existentialism, as has happened most noticeably with Bultmann and Tillich. In both instances, there is an insistence that the experiencing subject cannot be submerged in the whole. For conservative theology, a person's objective redemption in Christ has to have a personal and subjective appropriation. Christ's work of achieving salvation is not separated from his later work of applying it through the Spirit to the individual. The existential theologians, of course, have a different way of articulating the personal element. The antithesis is not so much between being redeemed and unredeemed as between living an authentic and inauthentic existence. In inauthentic existence the experiencing subject is as dead to life as a drunkard is to his where-abouts. By contrast, a person lives authentically when he eschews the safe option of an unthinking existence and lays himself open to all possibilities. The personal element in both theologies is present although the reasons for its presence are different.

On the other hand, there are theologies which view salvation more corporately. The liberation and secular theologies begin with the premise that God has already saved society and both are opposed to the notion of a 'private' or personal faith. Indeed, theologies which make any use of the mystical theory of the atonement have a strong tendency in this direction because of the Platonic ideas which are at work, principally that Christ in the man Jesus joined himself to universal humanity. But even in traditional Roman Catholicism, which has never felt much affinity with the mystical theory, there is also a strong corporate element. God saved the Church which he founded on Peter and to it he has given unique powers. One is saved, not so much through the activity of the self in appropriating the truth of Christ, as by assenting to be a part of the corporate Church. What constitutes the corporate element ranges, therefore, from the Church in traditional Roman Catholicism to the whole of society in liberation theology, and the concern with the personal aspect of faith is in inverse proportion to the emphasis placed in the corporate.

Common concerns and divergent problems

Great as have been the differences between conservatives as exponents of a dogmatic theology, and those who are working within an apologetic framework, they all share a common concern growing out of their common problem. If that problem is the incompatibility of Christian faith with modernity, they are concerned that Christianity will no longer be treated seriously.

This is the fate of every half-believed *credo*. The incontrovertible truth we can believe whole-heartedly and, if necessary, proclaim with passion. The patent error, such as pagan myths and ancient divinities, we study assiduously and with insatiable curiosity. But the twilight belief, that which is neither incontrovertibly right nor patently wrong, falls into a category by itself, one which is best handled neither by serious attention nor by concentrated study but simply by being ignored. And that could become the fate of Christian belief.

Starting from this apprehension, apologetic theologies have moved to make accommodations to modernity, to graft Christian faith onto the self-consciousness of the secular person, so that in this way it will become an irremovable appendage. Dogmatic theologies, by contrast, see this as doomed from the start, not only because it generally fails to reckon with human rebellion, but because what is grafted on no longer represents the faith proclaimed in the Bible. Instead, dogmatic theologies take much more seriously the breach between God and man and accept as one of the hard facts of life that, apart from the Spirit, saving faith cannot be generated. For dogmatic theologies, the question of relating Christian faith to the modern world does not, therefore, present itself as a challenge in harmonization or accommodation but rather in confrontation and antithesis. Some will say that this is neither the way to win friends nor to influence people, that it is in fact a self-defeating approach. Others will reply that salvation must be

171

proclaimed on God's terms and that it ought to be remembered that to men, God's wisdom often does look like foolishness. Especially is this so when we are talking about the cross.

Consequently, dogmatic and apologetic theologies have divergent problems. The strength of the former, it seems, is the weakness of the latter and the strength of the latter is the weakness of the former. Dogmatic theologies have earned the right to be heard for what they have to say about biblical doctrine; apologetic theologies have established their right to speak about the contemporary world. The one has explored the mind of the biblical authors, the other the mind of modern man. Is it beyond the bounds of hope that each might learn from the other?

This does not imply that anyone may lay claim to infallible interpretation, either of God or of man, but rather it seeks to recognize the help that might be given in finding ways of building bridges with a firm biblical support on one end to the modern world, perceptively and sensitively understood, on the other end. It is not enough to have right doctrine; it is not enough to have perceptive theology. The former without the latter is like a limp root dangling out of heaven which never makes contact with the earth; the latter without the former is like a soaring mountain which, if it is occasionally obscured in cloud, nevertheless always fails to penetrate heaven itself. The one is divine language which is uninterpreted; the other is human language which is ineffective.

The two mediating theologies which have been considered, neo-orthodoxy and Roman Catholicism, are interesting for their fusion of dogmatic and apologetic elements. It is not surprising, perhaps, that both have been caught in some rather withering crossfire. In the case of neo-orthodoxy, criticism came from many conservatives on the one side because they perceived in it elements of the apologetic methodology; criticism came from the other side, however, from the existentialist and secular theologians, because of their restiveness with dogmatic verities. Exactly the same pattern is currently being duplicated in Roman Catholicism and only time will tell whether it will be with the same results.

What is in fact desired is not a *via media,* a negotiated compromise, between the opposing mentalities. Neither side will be content to surrender what it rightly regards as its strength. But this does not mean that each is unable to complement its own strength by that of the opposite approach.

This, however, would appear to be an easier task for conservatives than for those in the existential, secular and liberation theologies. The wholly insubstantial grasp of the modern world which conservatives sometimes display must give way to a serious wrestling with those problems that have engaged others. The contemporary mind will have to be sensitively delineated afresh, the undercurrents of secularism charted, the structures of power analysed, the assumptions of our culture measured. The world does not stand still for the people of God, nor will it do for them the hard work which they must do for themselves. And that hard work is what (for want of a better word) incarnates God's truth in each age. Christian faith does not change; its relationship to the world does. If conservatives have been generally right in the way they have understood the Bible, they have often failed to engage it with the cogs of their time. The task is not so much that of finding new truth in the Bible, but of finding new ways of making it truth for *our world.*

By contrast, apologetic theologies are sometimes strikingly perceptive about the modern world, but they view the Bible through a subjective prism and therefore see only a distortion of what is there. If conservative theology needs to be immersed in the world, apologetic theologies need to be emancipated from it, and that is a more painful and difficult task. Conservatives are right to attempt to interpret biblical doctrine from within a biblical world-view but mistaken when they imagine that they themselves live in that world. Apologetic theologies have candidly owned the world which is ours but are mistaken in thinking that it also belonged to the apostles. Each indulges in myth, each is pursuing its separate and diverging path and each is making it easy for the world to ignore Christian faith. It should not be so. It need not be so. By God's grace, it will not be so.

Index